GERMANY'S
FIRST BID FOR COLONIES
1884–1885

A J. P. TAYLOR is a Research Fellow of Magdalen College, Oxford, and head of the Beaverbrook Library in London. He is the author of many books, including *The Origins of the Second World War, Politics in Wartime,* and *English History, 1914-1945.*

GERMANY'S
FIRST BID FOR COLONIES

1884–1885

A MOVE IN
BISMARCK'S EUROPEAN POLICY

BY

A. J. P. TAYLOR

The Norton Library
W · W · NORTON & COMPANY · INC ·
NEW YORK

First published in the Norton Library 1970

SBN 393 00530 5

Books That Live

The Norton imprint on a book means that in the publisher's
estimation it is a book not for a single season but for the years.

W. W. Norton & Company, Inc.

PRINTED IN THE UNITED STATES OF AMERICA

1 2 3 4 5 6 7 8 9 0

CONTENTS

INTRODUCTION

THIRTY years of European concussions came to an end at the Congress of Berlin. In the ensuing period the European powers shrank from European conflicts, and the problems which continued to divide them were, as the French said of Alsace-Lorraine, " reserved for the future ". European rivalries were temporarily diverted to the less dangerous field of extra-European expansion, and in the years between 1881 and 1912 the European powers extended their influence or their empires over Africa and large parts of Asia.

This imperialist expansion was of two kinds. The more important was the struggle for the heritage of decaying states, themselves very often the relics of earlier epochs of imperialism. The struggle over the succession to the Turkish Empire had gone on since the end of the seventeenth century; but what distinguished the " Age of Imperialism " was that more of these decadent states came into the market and that the process of absorption was rendered more and more difficult by the interference of some other European (and in one case of an Asiatic) power. Thus France was able to establish her control over Tunis, Annam, and Madagascar without serious difficulty; but she extended her influence over Morocco only after coming twice to the brink of war with Germany. Great Britain annexed the Boer republics (relic of an earlier Dutch empire) after a period of conflict with Germany; and she asserted her predominance in Egypt after a period of conflict with France. It was owing to the rivalry of England and Russia that Persia and Afghanistan preserved their independence—though Persia nearly lost it to Russia in the last years before 1914; and, thanks to the jealousy of all the powers, China preserved her independence, except for the loss of a few ports in what proved to be an abortive partition in 1898. It is not necessary to speculate at length on the reasons for these imperialist activities : the objects of conflict were going concerns ; their economic and political importance was known ; and in many cases they adjoined possessions or strategic routes of European powers (Morocco on the frontier of Algiers, Egypt and Persia on the route to India, the Boer republics on the frontier of Cape Colony, and so on). The rival powers were still primarily influenced by European considerations ; and though the extra-European questions provoked crises, it was the old problem of the Balkans which produced the War of 1914, with the even older problem of the Franco-German frontier as a contributory cause.

The predominance of European considerations is even greater in relation to the second form of European expansion in these thirty years—the occupation of hitherto ownerless territories, or rather of territories with no ruler substantial enough to be treated as an independent power. Under this head come most of Africa and the islands of the Pacific. The enormous areas of tropical Africa appear impressive on the map ; but of most of them the plain truth is that they had remained so long ownerless because they were not worth owning. The principal exception was the basin of the Congo, which, curiously enough, slipped through the hands of the two traditional colonial powers, England and France, and was secured by a royal speculator, Leopold II. of Belgium, masquerading as a philanthropic society. Portugal, with a shadowy traditional claim to all Africa, managed to retain one colony on the west coast, and one on the east. France, who created a great North African empire within a few years, had intelligible political reasons for doing so : the republican government wished to demonstrate by colonial expansion that France was still a great power despite the humiliations of 1870 ; part of the expansion was undertaken to protect the frontiers of the existing colony of Algiers; and much of the rest aimed at opening for France an overland route to the Sudan, where —it was commonly believed—it would be possible to divert the upper Nile and so make the English position in Egypt untenable. France regarded Egypt as part of the heritage of Napoleon, and, in endeavouring to oust the English, was seeking to recover what had once been hers.

England had two interests in Africa, which she meant to preserve—a settlement of British colonists in South Africa, and a predominant influence in Egypt, which was both valuable in itself and a vital point on the route to India. The new English acquisitions were made in order to protect what England already possessed by cutting off the Nile from foreign interference, and the Boer republics, the neighbours of Cape Colony, from foreign help. It is true that these new possessions sometimes proved to have a value of their own, such as the diamond mines of Kimberley and the cotton plantations of the Sudan; but it was not for this that they had been undertaken.

In these years of " the scramble for Africa " there was suddenly added to the old colonial rivals, France and England, a power which had hitherto confined itself strictly to the European continent. The German colonial empire, or rather the formulation of its theoretical claims, was virtually the work of a single year: the Cameroons were established in July 1884, German South-West Africa in August, New Guinea in December 1884, and German East Africa was begun in May 1885 (though its frontiers were not settled until 1890); Samoa was added in 1899; otherwise—apart from some minor adjustments of the Cameroons frontier at the expense of France after the second Moroccan crisis (1911)—the German colonial empire was complete. The success of Germany, as previously of Prussia, had been due to freedom from all concern in non-German questions: Prussia had been able to secure the support of Russia because of her indifference to the Near East, and of Italy, because of her indifference to the maintenance of the treaty settlement of Europe. It is therefore surprising that Germany should have deliberately pushed her way into the hornets' nest of colonial conflicts. The explanation of this German outburst of colonial activity has usually been found in the rising enthusiasm for colonies, and it is true that there was in Germany a certain amount of colonial agitation. Imperial Germany was a " made " state, an artificial reproduction of French nationalism tinged with echoes from the Holy Roman Empire; the new Germany had no political tradition, and had therefore to ape the political traditions of others. Many Germans demanded a colonial empire simply because other great powers had colonial empires, and their demand was reinforced by the current belief that the possession of colonies was in itself a profitable thing. Many writers, not only German, at this time failed to grasp the truth about the British empire—that it had come into being as the result of British commercial enterprise and industrial success ; and they asserted the reverse, that the prosperity and wealth of Great Britain were due to the existence of her empire. The German campaign for colonies rested on the simple dogma—give Germany colonies and the Germans will then be as prosperous as the English.

It is difficult to believe that this primitive outlook was shared by the German government, particularly in the days of Bismarck. It has often been suggested that Bismarck was driven into a policy of colonial expansion against his will. Lord Sanderson, who was a member of the British Foreign Office in 1884, put forward this explanation in a defence of Bismarck written some twenty years later : " Prince Bismarck was personally opposed to German colonisation. . . . He therefore encouraged us to make fresh annexations on the West Coast of Africa, to which we had been previously indisposed : hoping that the clamour for such annexations by Germany would subside. Suddenly he found that the movement was too strong for him, and that his only expedient, in order to avoid a crushing Parliamentary defeat, was to make friends with the party which urged the acquisition of Colonies. He went to Lord Ampthill [the British Ambassador], explained his dilemma, said he should have to take up the Colonial policy vigorously, and begged that we should give him our support." [1]

To imagine that Bismarck was influenced by public opinion, or that he was swayed by fear of " a crushing parliamentary defeat " is to transfer to Germany the conceptions of constitutional government as practised in England or France. The Imperial German government did not depend upon a parliamentary majority, and the German press was only slightly freer than the press in Russia. There are, of course, plenty of instances—the history of the Schleswig-Holstein affair is full of them—when Bismarck gave the signal for a popular campaign to compel him to do what he wanted to do, but there seems to be no other case in which Bismarck is supposed to have bowed to the force of public opinion. Nor is it conceivable that Bismarck was suddenly converted, after years of scepticism, to a belief in the value of colonies. He was contemptuous enough of those who were ready to disturb the quiet of Europe for the sake of the " sheep-stealers " of the Balkans. But even Bismarck could not have found words of condemnation strong enough for a policy which provoked a quarrel with Great Britain for the sake of the " light soil " of South-West Africa or of the head-hunters of New Guinea.

It is the purpose of the following chapters to discover

[1] Sanderson, Observations of Feb. 21, 1907. *British Documents on the Origins of the War* (cited B.D.), vol. iii. p. 422. There is no contemporary evidence for this alleged conversation between Ampthill and Bismarck. Sanderson's memory was not very accurate, as is shown by his further remarks : " We countermanded some projects, but in other places we had already gone too far and could not draw back, and where Cape Colony was concerned we could do little in the way of concession ". The exact opposite is the case.

an explanation of Bismarck's colonial policy by fitting it
into the structure of contemporary European politics. His
colonial policy alone seems meaningless and irrational;
but when to the relations of England and Germany are
added those of Germany and France, and those of France
and England, Bismarck's policy in 1884 and 1885 becomes
as purposeful as at any other time in his career. Such an
examination shows that Bismarck quarrelled with England
in order to draw closer to France; and that the method of
quarrel was the deliberately provocative claim to ownerless lands, in which the German government had hitherto
shown no interest. These lands had a certain negative
value to Great Britain, in that they adjoined existing
British colonies or lay near British strategic routes; but
their value was not such as to provoke the English government into a war. Moreover, they were of no concern to any
other power, and claims to them would not cause any international complications, such as would have been occasioned
by German demands in China or Persia. The German
colonies were the accidental by-product of an abortive
Franco-German entente.

It may be asked whether the later colonial disputes and
discussions between England and Germany were similarly
related to the European situation. It would be rash to attempt to discover in German policy after 1890 any such
persistent and successful planning as in the days of Bismarck, particularly when to the gross incompetence of his
successors were added the planless impulses of William II.
Moreover, with the passing of time the German colonies
did acquire a spurious ideological value; they became a
white elephant, a sacred relic of Bismarck's era. He could
contemplate passing on their useless burden to England, and
even in 1890 the German government could surrender vast
theoretical claims in East Africa in exchange for the really
valuable island of Heligoland. Ten years later the value of
colonies was taken as an axiom by the Germans, and from

the failure of their colonial ventures they drew the moral not that colonies were a mistaken luxury, but that they ought to have more, and better, colonies. In the first decade of the twentieth century the Germans demanded " a place in the sun " ; by this they meant someone else's place in the sun, their own having proved too hot.

Nevertheless the connection between colonial questions and the European situation remained as close as ever. A detailed study of this later period will be possible only when the publication of the French documents is complete and when more British material is available ; but certain general tendencies are already obvious. The men of the " New Course ", who succeeded Bismarck in 1890, believed that his policy of preventing a Russian attack upon Austria-Hungary by German friendship with Russia had failed, and that a war in the Near East was inevitable ; their principal anxiety was therefore to secure English support for Austria—if possible by including England in the Triple Alliance—and the remaining colonial questions were speedily settled in a sense favourable to England. English policy did not, however, move in the anticipated direction : Salisbury would not go beyond the agreements of 1887, and even these were virtually abandoned by the Liberal government of 1892. By 1894 the Germans were losing patience ; they determined to show England that, unless she was more forthcoming towards Austria, she could no longer count on German complacency in colonial questions. The result was the German opposition to the Anglo-Congolese treaty of May 12, 1894, which was accompanied by the first attempt at Franco-German co-operation since the fall of Bismarck.

The Anglo-Congolese treaty was undoubtedly a very badly managed affair. The Liberal government, some members of which wished to withdraw from Egypt altogether, could not possibly undertake the reconquest of the Sudan, which was in the hands of the dervishes ; fearing a French advance to the Sudan overland, it now proposed to lease to the Congo Free State the western gateway to the Sudan, the Bahr-el-Ghazal (which was in the power of the dervishes and which belonged, if it belonged to anyone, to Egypt), and thus interpose a neutral barrier between France and the Nile. A more absurd attempt at imperialism on the cheap could not easily be imagined; and to make matters worse, compensation for the lease of the mythical British rights over the Bahr-el-Ghazal was found in a lease to Great Britain of a strip of Congolese territory from the frontier of Uganda to the northern end of Lake Tanganyika. This strip was on the borders of German East Africa and the Germans therefore claimed that they were being " encircled " by British territory; the clause was not an essential part of the treaty and there is no doubt that the Germans could have secured its abandonment by a direct approach to London. But the Germans wished to teach the English a lesson and proposed to the French, who had much more serious reasons for opposing the treaty, that the two countries should co-operate on the basis of maintaining the *status quo* as established by the Congo Act of 1885. The French accepted the proposal eagerly; in fact this moment, when France was concentrating all her energies on the struggle for Egypt and when a French success in Egypt seemed likely, was the most favourable opportunity that ever occurred for Franco-German co-operation. But to the men of the " New Course " fear of France was at this time little more than a Bismarckian ghost story and their sole concern was in the Near East; at the next interview the French ambassador was told that Germany having got what she wanted—the cancelling of the clause objectionable to her—the Germans had changed their mind as to the desirability of Franco-German co-operation.

The result of this policy was the reverse of what the Germans expected—England became not more, but less, friendly to the powers of the Triple Alliance. Rosebery attempted to co-operate in the Near East with Russia and France, and Salisbury, on his return to office in 1895, displayed alarming signs of being prepared to partition the Turkish Empire with Russia—to the detriment, as the Germans believed, of Austria and Italy. The Germans therefore reverted to Bismarck's idea of a continental league, partly with the intention of teaching England a lesson, but even more in the hope of settling European rivalries at England's expense. The excuse for the German change of policy was the Jameson raid, which led to an open demonstration of German hostility to England in the Kruger telegram of January 3, 1896. The basis of the German policy was a division of the world, by which France should receive the Congo Free State, Russia Corea, and Germany some Chinese port ; Italy's protectorate of Abyssinia would be recognised, and Austria would receive from Russia a guarantee of the *status quo* in the Near East.[1] Such a scheme, apart from its crudity of detail, had something Bismarckian about it ; but Bismarck would have realised its fatal flaw. Only the prospect of support concerning Egypt, such as Bismarck had offered France in 1884 and 1885, would tempt France into a continental coalition; but Egypt was expressly omitted from the proposal, in order to play off England against France at a later date. Bismarck could have told his successors that the only way to achieve results with a policy is to behave as if you meant it whole-heartedly. The reservation concerning Egypt destroyed any effect the Kruger telegram might have had upon the French, who used the opportunity of Anglo-German friction to open negotiations with England (as it proved, unsuccessful negotiations) for a settlement of the Egyptian question. The policy of the Kruger telegram annoyed the English without reconciling the French.

[1] Memorandum by Holstein, Dec. 30, 1895. *Die Grosse Politik* (cited G.P.), vol. xi. No. 2640, pp. 67-9.

In 1896 the Germans were no more successful than before in securing English backing for Austria in the Near East; but the Austro-Russian agreement of May 1897 placed the Eastern question on ice for eleven years and so put an end to German anxieties. Henceforth Germany aimed at preserving a free hand; she would make no binding alliance with France and Russia on the one side, nor with Great Britain on the other, but would make occasional agreements with each side as an indication of her superior position. The controversy over the future of the Portuguese colonies is a case in point. Early in 1898 Portugal was in a difficult financial position, and it was generally expected that she would try to raise a loan on the security of her colonies ; England was temporarily on good terms with France as the result of the agreement over the frontiers of Nigeria, and it looked as though she would take the opportunity to extend her control over the Portuguese colonies, in view of their strategic importance in relation to South Africa. The Germans protested, and they also enquired in Paris whether France would welcome a practical co-operation with Germany in individual questions as they arose. The moment for the enquiry was ill-chosen; a ministerial crisis was proceeding in Paris, as the result of which Hanotaux was replaced by Delcassé. Hanotaux is said to have responded favourably, but he was already out of office ; the enquiry was not repeated to Delcassé, and he did not choose to reply to the earlier one or did not know of its existence. The Germans assumed, probably correctly, that Delcassé preferred the policy of co-operation with England, which had been expressed in the Nigerian agreement, and they determined to show the French that Germany could always outbid them for English friendship. The English were therefore driven into making an agreement for the hypothetical partition of the Portuguese colonies ; the agreement had no practical importance, as Portugal managed to scrape through without mortgaging the colonies, which did not therefore come on to the market, but it served its purpose of giving the French a warning.

At the height of the Fashoda crisis Delcassé seems to have put out feelers for German support against England, but apparently he made Franco-German co-operation conditional on autonomy, or something like it, for Alsace-Lorraine ; and this proposal had no attraction for the Germans, who expected Anglo-French relations to become still worse and could therefore wait for an unconditional French offer. During 1899 it became increasingly obvious that the conflict in South Africa would end in a war between Great Britain and the Boer republics. The Germans, despite their previous assurance that the Portuguese agreement of 1898 had put an end to their claim to interfere in South Africa, at once found another cause of conflict with Great Britain; they demanded that the Samoan archipelago, which was administered jointly by England, the United States, and Germany, should be partitioned, with Germany receiving the lion's share. The dispute was even more trivial than the dispute over New Guinea, which is described later in this book ; in the words of Richthofen, the German undersecretary, " The whole of Samoa was not worth the money spent upon telegrams to and from Apia ".[1] Its sole purpose, in fact, was to indicate to the French that Germany was quarrelling with England and would welcome proposals for Franco-German co-operation. Twice, in the course of October 1899, the idea of such co-operation was placed before the French ; but the French replies were not very encouraging, and the Germans learnt that the French were at this very time resisting the Russian proposal for a continental league against England. The Samoan question was therefore brought to a conclusion ; the English, with the Boer war on their hands, acquiesced in the German demands and the French were once more given a warning that Germany could outbid them for English friendship.

[1] Lascelles to Salisbury, Jan. 20, 1899. B.D. vol. i. No. 128, p. 109.

Surprisingly enough the Samoan affair was the last colonial dispute between England and Germany. Between 1900 and 1904 European relations were overshadowed by the question of the future of the Chinese Empire, which entered an acute stage with the Boxer rebellion of 1900, and in 1904 the value of colonial disputes for Germany was destroyed by the Anglo-French entente. Germany could no longer offer to join France in a common hostility to England; and she could no longer demonstrate her superior ability to return to good relations with England. Henceforth the object of German policy was to prove to the French that England was an unreliable friend. The menacing attitude adopted by Germany over Morocco in 1905 avowedly aimed at destroying the Anglo-French entente by showing that England would not help France in a crisis ; the result was the direct opposite—that England began military conversations with France and that the two countries drew much closer than had ever been contemplated by the makers of the entente in 1904.[1] The German attempt to separate England and France was repeated in the second Moroccan crisis, the crisis of Agadir, and ended with an even more emphatic failure.

Having failed to shake the entente by threats to France, the Germans attempted in 1912 to sap it by soft words to England. English unfriendliness to Germany was blamed for the tension in Europe, which English public opinion felt so acutely, and the British government were called upon to restore good relations by colonial concessions. The British government knew that any agreement with Germany would be quoted by the Germans to the French as evidence that England was an unreliable friend; nevertheless for the sake of English opinion they allowed themselves

[1] As late as November 1903 the French tried to smuggle into the entente agreements a clause designed to prevent British fortification of the Balearics, a striking illustration of their view as to the future of Anglo-French relations.

to be drawn into a discussion of German colonial grievances. The abortive agreement of 1898 for the partition of the Portuguese colonies was brought up to date by assigning a still larger share to Germany, and preparations were made for partitioning the Belgian Congo on a similar basis. The Germans were not made more pacific by this prospect of a further " place in the sun " ; they were merely convinced that British attachment to the ententes was weakening and were therefore encouraged to adopt a bellicose policy in July 1914.

The Germans, it must be admitted, made the most of these rather trivial colonial disputes. Yet the persistence with which they sought to convince France of the superior advantages of German friendship was in reality completely futile. The Holstein-Bülow policy of supporting France with reserves had no chance of success ; but, as the later chapters of this book show, nor had Bismarck's policy of co-operating with France without reserves. So long as the shadow of Alsace-Lorraine lay between France and Germany, a reconciliation was impossible. Bismarck did his best to undo the mistake of 1871 by apologising for it, but that was hardly enough, and subsequent governments did not even apologise. French hostility to Germany was the one permanent factor in the ever-changing combinations of European diplomacy; this fatal weakness in Germany's diplomatic position enabled Italy and Austria, powers so much weaker than Germany, to exact German compliance to their wildest schemes. If Germany had enjoyed a real security on her western frontier, would she have tolerated the Italian attack on Turkey in 1912, and would she have been ready to risk her own existence as a great power for the sake of Austro-Hungarian hegemony in the Balkans ?

The directors of British policy had some vague conception of this German weakness, and they were never so shaken by the threat of a Franco-German entente or of a continental coalition as the Germans thought they ought to have been. On the other hand they had a weakness of their own, which prevented their taking up a firm attitude towards the far-fetched colonial claims of Germany : they suffered from a guilty conscience. The average Englishman was ashamed of the British Empire and believed (quite wrongly) that it had been acquired in some wicked fashion; " peccavi ", Napier's announcement of the conquest of Scinde, could be taken as device for the Empire as a whole. The apparent exception, the aggressive Imperialism of the late nineteenth century, was merely part of the Diabolism of the Naughty Nineties, with Chamberlain as the Oscar Wilde of politics.

This sense of sin placed British governments at a dis-advantage in their negotiations with Germany: they were convinced of the justice of the German grievances even before the grievances were expressed. British governments had spent most of the nineteenth century trying to prevent the growth of the British Empire, and still it had grown ; German governments had done their utmost to encourage colonial enterprise, and yet their empire was a failure ; clearly it was the fault of British governments and they must put it right. Of course they wanted to put it right with-out annoying the colonial governments or the British public; there they stood, ears anxiously cocked for the next German complaint. Moreover, British politicians have al-ways been peculiarly sensitive to the charge of "unfriendli-ness " towards other politicians or other countries. The atmosphere of the House of Commons usually prevents these personal antipathies at home (the sensation caused by Parnell was due to his disregard of the House of Commons convention), and British statesmen have always sought to reduce foreign relations to the same intimate level. Granville's letters to Herbert Bismarck—my dear fellow, what can be wrong ?—are not unique in the record of British policy, and if the dear fellow insists on this or that as the price of renewing eternal friendship, of course he must have it. Anglo-German relations between 1884 and 1914 abound in these private letters and unofficial visits, culminating in another British surrender and renewed protestations of friendship. But in the last years before 1914 British politicians were beginning to realise that only one thing could end these quarrels and secure German friendship for ever— the adoption of a policy which would give the Germans what they called security, but what to others appeared as German hegemony over the entire continent of Europe. Even Gladstone and Granville would have been unwilling to buy German friendship at this price.

CHAPTER I

BISMARCK'S APPROACH TO FRANCE,
DECEMBER 1883–APRIL 1884

ALL that Germany asked after the victories of 1866 and
1870 was to be left alone; she was, in Metternich's phrase,
a satiated power, and Bismarck's policy from 1871 to
1890 had one object only—to keep Europe quiet. The two
principal dangers to the peace of Europe were an aggressive Russian policy in the Near East, which might lead
to a war between Russia and Austria, and a French attempt
to reverse the verdict of 1870 by an attack upon Germany.
Bismarck's policy in regard to Russia has been the subject
of many books, his policy towards France has been less
carefully examined.[1] The most obvious part of Bismarck's
policy was to prevent France's securing assistance against
Germany. Alliance between France and an anti-German
Austria-Hungary was forestalled by the Austro-German
alliance of 1879; a period of estrangement between Germany
and Russia was brought to an end with the renewal of the
League of the Three Emperors in 1881; French neglect of
Italy (a neglect shared by Bismarck) drove Italy into
making the Triple Alliance in 1882.

A less obvious element in Bismarck's policy was his
anxiety not to drive the French to despair. With allies
France might attack Germany, because she saw some prospect of success; without allies France might resort to the
extremity of war even with the certainty of being defeated.
Bismarck's problem was to find for France friends who

[1] Bismarck's policy has been described from rather a different
angle in P. B. Mitchell, *The Bismarckian Policy of Conciliation with
France, 1875–1885* (Philadelphia, 1935).

would be safe friends, because they would not be anti-German. Bismarck thought he had discovered the solution in co-operation between England and France. England could be relied on not to support France in an anti-German policy, and France would not encourage England's hostility to Russia, which was the one flaw in her pacifism. In furtherance of this Anglo-French entente Bismarck encouraged the two powers to co-operate in the occupation of Egypt, when the Egyptian question became acute in 1882. This proposal had disastrous results : at the last minute the French government was compelled by French public opinion to withdraw, the English went on alone, and the British government managed by a series of mistakes to transform Egypt into a subject for the most violent conflict between the two countries.

The balance of Bismarck's policy was thus destroyed. In the first stages of the conflict over Egypt he supported England against France, but it was soon obvious to him that he would never secure in return any English support for Germany in Europe. It was not safe to leave France isolated ; the only remaining alternative was to offer France the friendship of Germany. After all, Austria had become the ally of Germany, despite the defeat of 1866 ; why should not France now become the ally of Germany, despite the defeat and memories of 1870 ? But to the German mind friendship with one power necessarily implies hostility against another, and Germany, to make herself presentable to France, had to provoke a quarrel with England so that Franco-German friendship should have the solid foundation of anglophobia. An essential condition for such a policy was friendship between Russia and Austria ; for a bellicose Russia would attempt to outbid Germany in courting France, and a menaced Austria would need the support of England. Between 1881 and 1885 Russia and Austria were on tolerable, if not good, terms for the only time between 1875 and 1897, and Bismarck was therefore free to conduct his experiment with the western powers.

Bismarck did not, of course, plump for France ; his method was to keep open alternative lines of policy and take the credit for whichever one succeeded. In these years the major theme was friendship with France, based on hostility to England ; but there was also the minor theme of friendship with England—at a price—based on renewed hostility to France. The simultaneous pursuit of two contradictory policies was for Bismarck nothing new, as may be seen by a comparison with his policy before 1866. In this instance Bismarck aimed at war against Austria with the good-will of France ; but until the very last moment he never excluded the alternative of war against France in alliance with Austria ; had Austrian statesmen been less arrogant or more far-sighted, the famous sentence in Bismarck's *Reflections and Reminiscences* might have run : "From the day of my appointment to office I worked for an alliance with Austria and a war against France ". It would be paying any ordinary statesman an undeserved compliment to explain his every action as part of a deep-laid plan ; but Bismarck was not an ordinary statesman. The nervous irritability, from which he was undoubtedly suffering in these years, may explain his frequent loss of temper ; but it does not explain why he usually lost his temper with the English and not with the French. In Sir Eyre Crowe's words, " To assume that so great a statesman was not quite clear as to the objects of his policy would be the *reductio ad absurdum* of any hypothesis ".

The two ideas of hostility to England (though as yet only in the form of personal dislike of Gladstone) and co-operation with France seem to have been first expressed by Bismarck on May 13, 1883, in a conversation with the French minister, Waddington, who stopped at Berlin on his way to represent France at the coronation of Alexander

III.[1] A conversation of this kind is not perhaps so significant as one with the regular French representative, and Bismarck would naturally emphasise the advantages of friendship with Germany to an envoy who was on his way to demonstrate French friendship with Russia. It was not until the autumn of 1883, when the Anglo-French quarrel over Egypt had obviously become permanent, that Bismarck began to emphasise his desire for friendship with France. Prince Hohenlohe, the German ambassador at Paris, was charged with a friendly message to the French government,[2] which he delivered on November 5, and when Courcel, the French ambassador at Berlin, expressed his gratitude, he was at once invited to visit Bismarck at Friedrichsruhe despite Bismarck's ill-health—a very unusual honour.[3] The ostensible topic of conversation during Courcel's visit on December 11 was the French advance in Tonkin, but Bismarck took the opportunity of complaining that the attitude of the French press made it difficult for him to be as friendly to France as he would like. Courcel was treated in a particularly amiable manner; he wrote, "Throughout my visit I was the object of the most delicate attentions and I had to resist the most friendly pressure to remain a second night and a third day under this hospitable roof". Bismarck was especially insistent on his appreciation of Ferry, the French Prime Minister, and said to Courcel as he was leaving: "I do not cheat at cards nor do I cheat in politics. I believe that the first duty and the first interest of the diplomat is to inspire confidence in his word ; otherwise he loses his principal means of action. I do not know M. Ferry personally ; but tell him that my good-will towards him is sincere and that my policy

---

[1] Waddington to Challemel-Lacour, May 14, 1883. *Documents Diplomatiques Français* (cited D.D.F.), 1st series, vol. v. No. 35, pp. 38-42.

[2] G.P. vol. iii. p. 409, n. 1.

[3] G.P. vol. iii. No. 677, and p. 409, n. 2.

towards him will not change; I hope that his, too, will not change towards me." [1] Ferry's policy of colonial expansion certainly depended on German tolerance, but Ferry and Courcel were rather taken aback at this emphatic display of affection on Bismarck's part. They surmised that Bismarck was working to keep France and Russia apart in preparation for a war against Russia in 1884; but in fact negotiations for the renewal of the League of the Three Emperors were far advanced, and it is therefore obvious that Bismarck was planning not a war with Russia but a quarrel with England.

To find the ground for such a quarrel was by no means easy, for the interests of England and Germany were nowhere in conflict. The dominant problem in British foreign policy at this time was Egypt, which had been occupied by the British in 1882. The Gladstone government was prevented by its liberal principles from annexing Egypt, and had therefore to pose as the mandatory of the powers —no easy feat when one of the powers, France, strongly objected to the English occupation and another, Russia, opposed England on general grounds. Lord Granville, the foreign secretary, was elderly, he was ill, and he had serious financial worries; he had originally been appointed foreign secretary (in 1851) with the task of being polite to Queen Victoria after the quarrels between the Queen and Palmerston, and throughout his later activity as foreign secretary (1870 to 1874, and 1880 to 1885) *bonhomie* remained his stock-in-trade. That a foreign secretary should have a policy hardly occurred to him; he merely transferred to foreign affairs the principle on which Whig cabinets were

---

[1] The visit is described in Courcel to Ferry, confidential, Dec. 13, 1883. D.D.F. vol. v. No. 166, p. 170; Courcel to Ferry, very confidential, Dec. 14, 1883. D.D.F. vol. v. No. 168, pp. 173-7; Courcel to Ferry, private and confidential letter, Dec. 16, 1883. D.D.F. vol. v. No. 170, pp. 178-81; and Courcel to Ferry, private, Dec. 31 1883. D.D.F. vol. v. No. 180, pp. 190-93.

held together—personal friendship. His sole endeavour was to be polite and considerate, in the hope that no foreign government would be so cruel as to oppose the wishes of a benevolent old gentleman.

When the difficulties over Egypt made it necessary for England to secure German support, Granville applied his usual method ; he went out of his way to be exceptionally kind to Bismarck's son, Herbert, who was at that time first secretary at the London embassy. Herbert Bismarck was, for example, the only secretary of embassy ever invited to dinner at Windsor; Granville often entertained him at Walmer ; and much business was done with Herbert Bismarck, which would normally have concerned Münster, the German ambassador. The two old Whigs, Granville and Ampthill, the ambassador at Berlin, were very pleased with their ingenuity ; [1] but it is doubtful whether their policy was really wise. Bismarck, not being a Whig, did not base his policy on family considerations and was unaffected by Granville's flattery of his son. Herbert Bismarck was young and very arrogant ; he carried on these private negotiations in a very slip-shod way, of which it was impossible to complain as it would have been if the discussions had been more regular, and he had all his father's rudeness without his ability. Moreover, Herbert Bismarck had a personal reason for wishing to discredit his chief, Münster, and anything which the British government did through Münster: Herbert wished to become Secretary of State in place of Count Hatzfeldt, who, it was known, would prefer a comfortable embassy. Some German ambassador had therefore to be forced out of his post, and Münster was the most suitable victim. It is quite probable that the elder Bismarck did not

[1] Ampthill to Granville, private, Feb. 3, 1883. Granville Papers (cited G.D.), G.D. 29/178 : "Never was your kindness politically better invested and I chuckle in my sleeve when I hear people marvel at Bismarck's growing preference for England and steady faith in the foreign policy of Her Majesty's liberal advisers ".

appreciate his son's personal motive and accepted the
criticisms of Münster in all good faith.[1]

It would have been simple for Bismarck to stage a quarrel
with the English, merely by joining the French opposition
in regard to Egypt; but this would not have served his
purpose, which was to convince the French that he had
grievances of his own and therefore actually needed French
help. A grievance had to be created, and Bismarck turned
to the colonial topics, which he had hitherto despised.
There had been a certain amount of colonial agitation in
Germany in the preceding years, but Ampthill had always
reported, no doubt correctly, that Bismarck was entirely
opposed to colonial expansion and that the agitation would
never succeed so long as Bismarck remained in office.[2] The
German government was constantly being asked for its
protection by German traders all over the world, but all
that Bismarck would do was to give them the assistance of
the nearest German consul. In 1882 a rather disreputable
German trader, named Lüderitz, wished to establish himself at Angra Pequena, a port on the desolate west coast of
Africa some two hundred miles north of the Orange river,
which was the frontier of Cape Colony. The Cape exercised
jurisdiction over some of the islands off the coast, which
were useful in the trifling coastal trade, and in 1878 the
British government had occupied Walfish Bay, the only
good harbour between the Orange river and the Portuguese frontier at latitude 18°. But in 1880 the British
government had refused to protect some German mission-

---

[1] Münster managed to hold on to his position despite Herbert's best
efforts, and was only got rid of in November 1885, when he was moved
to Paris to succeed Prince Hohenlohe, who had become Governor of
Alsace-Lorraine. Hatzfeldt then became ambassador at London and
Herbert at last Secretary of State.

[2] *E.g.* Ampthill to Granville, No. 432, Sept. 18, 1880. F.O. 64/962;
No. 372, secret, Sept. 2, 1881. F.O. 64/983; No. 109, March 29, 1883.
F.O. 64/1026. Ampthill does not record any actual conversation with
Bismarck on the subject.

aries who had settled on the mainland. The Lüderitz proposal made Bismarck try again. On February 7, 1883,
Herbert Bismarck mentioned to Pauncefote, the Permanent
Under-Secretary, the establishment of a German trading
station at Angra Pequena and asked whether Great Britain
could protect it; "if not they [the German government]
will do their best to extend to it the same measure of protection which they give to their subjects in remote parts
of the world—but without having the least desire to establish any footing in South Africa ".[1] On February 22 Herbert
Bismarck was told that the British government would enquire of the Cape if British protection could be extended to
the German traders.

Nothing further happened until the summer, when
Lüderitz renewed his request for protection. He had in the
meantime bought at Angra Pequena a concession of in-
definite extent from a native chief, who according to the
information of the British Colonial Office had sold what did
not belong to him ; Lüderitz had then come into conflict
with a British trader, du Pass, who also claimed rights at
Angra Pequena, and he now sought German backing in his
quarrel. Bismarck had, as yet, no wish to start a conflict
with Great Britain and therefore approached the British
government for some definite reply with which he could
silence Lüderitz. On September 10, 1883, Plessen, the
German chargé d'affaires, enquired at the Foreign Office
if Great Britain had suzerainty at Angra Pequena and
" in case the suzerainty exists on what ground it rests ".
He also asked in the same unofficial manner " what view

---

[1] The documents concerning Angra Pequena in 1883 are in F.O.
64/1101. Many of these documents were published in the Blue Books ;
but a study of these, and of English opinion based upon them, would go
beyond the limits of the present subject. Bismarck's instruction to
Herbert Bismarck of Feb. 4, 1883, has now been published in W.O.
Aydelotte, " The First German Colony and its Diplomatic Conse-
quences ", *Cambridge Historical Journal*, vol. v. No. 3, p. 293.

Her Majesty's Government would take of the proceedings
of Lüderitz and whether they had any objection to them ".
Pauncefote, to whom the enquiry was addressed, had been
at the Colonial Office before he had moved over to the
Foreign Office, and he therefore knew the guiding principle
of British colonial policy at this time—that the Empire
was an intolerable nuisance and that it must not be extended. He saw no reason why England should undertake
the policing of a thousand miles of barren coast merely to
save Bismarck a little unpleasantness at home, still less
when the person seeking protection had the unsavoury
reputation of Lüderitz. Without consulting Granville he
drew up a Note some time in October for communication to
the German embassy, saying that " Her Majesty's Government have no claims or jurisdiction over the mainland ".
This Note was, however, never sent ; Pauncefote had overlooked the other principle of British colonial policy—that
the colonial governments must be kept in a good temper.
The Cape government did not want the expense of extending its authority ; but still less did it want German (or
any other) neighbours, who might disturb its native policy
or set up penal settlements.[1] Egged on by the Cape, the
Colonial Office decided to prevent any German settlement ;
the Germans were to be told that, although the district
was not British, Great Britain would object to its belonging to anybody else. This answer, slightly modified by the
Foreign Office, was passed on to Münster on November 21,
after he had on November 16 pressed for an answer to the
enquiry of September.[2]

[1] There is a good account of the relations between the Colonial
Office and the Cape government in R. I. Lovell, *The Struggle for South
Africa*. In regard to Anglo-German relations he tends to accept the
version first formulated by Thimme and since given a wider circulation
in W. L. Langer, *European Alliances and Alignments*.

[2] Granville to Münster, Nov. 21, 1884. F.O. 64/1101. The operative
sentence in the Colonial Office draft read : " It has always been understood that, although Her Majesty's Government have not proclaimed

This British answer was manifestly absurd, the unhappy result of the timid attitude observed towards the colonies by the Colonial Office ; the only thing to be said in its defence is that Bismarck had given no hint of intending to claim the area for Germany and that the Colonial Office imagined they had to provide him with some excuse with which to silence German colonial agitation. Instead they provided him with material for an Anglo-German quarrel. On December 21 (a fortnight after Courcel's visit to Friedrichsruhe) Münster brought to the Foreign Office a Note (the first official communication), in which it was pointed out that earlier British statements had repudiated any responsibility for the mainland, and which went on to enquire, if a claim was now made, on what title it rested and " what institutions England had there to give German traders such protection as would relieve the German government of the duty of protecting them itself ".[1] Bismarck claimed later that he knew England was not in a position to give any such protection and that he enquired only in order to have a negative answer on the files.[2] It seems a roundabout way of doing things, and it is more likely that Bismarck had not yet made up his mind what was to happen to Angra Pequena : if the French responded

the Queen's Sovereignty along the whole country . . . no foreign sove reignty and jurisdiction is admissible between the southern point of Portuguese jurisdiction at latitude 18° and the frontier of Cape Colony". This was modified by the Foreign Office to : " Although Her Majesty's Government have not proclaimed the Queen's sovereignty along the whole country . . . they consider that any claim of sovereignty or jurisdiction by a Foreign Power between the southern point of Portuguese jurisdiction at latitude 18° and the frontier of Cape Colony would infringe their legitimate rights ".

[1] German White Book on Angra Pequena, No. 9, quoted G.P. vol. iv. p. 56. G.P. does not publish any further documents about Angra Pequena, as the negotiations are, the editors say, known " im wesentlichen " from the White and Blue Books. It would, however, be rash to conclude that there are no further documents.

[2] Bismarck to Münster, June 10, 1884. White Book No. 24.

to his overture of December 11, then he had a quarrel with
England ready made ; if not, he hoped he would provoke
the British Government into forestalling the German
colonial enthusiasts whom he so much disliked. Herbert
Bismarck later alleged that Münster had added verbally
that experiences in Fiji (to which reference will be made
later) " made it desirable that we should take into our own
hands the protectorate of our fellow-countrymen in lands
as yet unannexed ".[1] But at almost the same time he
alleged the opposite—that Münster had asked Granville
whether England could not extend her protectorate to
Angra Pequena ; [2] there is no other evidence of either statement having been made, and it is safe to conclude that
both are on a par with many other of Herbert Bismarck's
allegations.

Certainly the Foreign Office showed no sign of having
been warned by Münster of any change in German policy.
Pauncefote did not mention the matter to Granville, and
indeed forgot all about it for a month. The affair was really
within the province of the Colonial Office, who had drafted
the unsatisfactory reply of November 21 ; at length, on
January 21, 1884, Pauncefote wrote to the Colonial Office
for an answer to Münster's Note of December 21. Lord
Derby, the Colonial Secretary, was a stronger man than
Lord Granville, but his strength was negative ; for him
policy meant inaction. Whereas Granville peered at the
world through a warm haze of benevolence, Derby saw it
with eyes sharpened by mistrust ; he believed that all and
sundry—his colleagues, foreign statesmen, colonial governments, and of course the Queen—were in a conspiracy to
compel him to do something unwelcome, and he was determined to thwart them by doing nothing at all. Granville,
to be sure, would always have been willing to pay black-

---

[1] Herbert Bismarck to Granville, June 19, 1884. G.D. 29/180.

[2] Herbert Bismarck to Bismarck, June 24, 1884. Rothfels, *Bismarcks englische Bundnispolitik*, p. 84.

mail in order to promote good feeling ; Derby would have ignored a blackmailing letter—along with all the rest of his correspondence. As Foreign Secretary in Disraeli's Cabinet, Derby had formulated his foreign policy in the remarkable phrase : " One can trust none of these governments " ; and this phrase, with the words " foreign or colonial " now added to it, represented his colonial policy.

Derby had left Disraeli's government rather than abandon his attitude of negation, and had joined Gladstone's government solely because he believed, and on the whole rightly, that the Liberal party had become the party of inaction. So far his career as Colonial Secretary had come up to his expectations—he had been able to renounce territory, to repudiate responsibility, to reiterate negatives. Now, so it appeared, he was being badgered both by the Germans and the Cape to extend responsibility and to undertake new expense ; for he naturally assumed that the prospect of colonial liabilities was as unwelcome to Bismarck as it was to himself. Lord Derby's obstinacy asserted itself. On February 3 he enquired of the Cape what answer was to be returned to Münster's Note of December 21 ; the Cape replied that it would like the territory annexed, but was not prepared to pay for its administration. Derby was not discouraged by this reply. There was shortly to be a general election at the Cape, and perhaps the new government would be less parsimonious ; or possibly the prospect of German action would frighten the Cape into generosity. At any rate, sooner or later somebody would have to act, and that somebody would not be the British Colonial Secretary ; at a waiting game Derby had few rivals. No answer was therefore returned by the Colonial Office to Pauncefote's enquiry, and in consequence no answer was returned by the Foreign Office to Münster. One thing is certain—the British government never for one moment contemplated forestalling the German colonial plans ; it was unaware that there were any German plans to forestall. As late as April 8

Ampthill commented on the report of a meeting of the German Colonial Society : " There is no reason to suppose that the German Government will be more disposed to lend its countenance to the efforts of the Society than it has been in the case of similar movements in the past ".[1]

There is nothing to suggest that at that moment Ampthill was wrong ; he was in close touch with German opinion and with Count Hatzfeldt, the secretary of state. Angra Pequena was never mentioned to him ; the first mutterings of the storm concerned not Africa, but the German land claims in Fiji. German traders had bought land from the native chiefs and had been dispossessed by the British authorities on the ground that the land belonged to the tribes ; Bismarck demanded a mixed commission to settle the issue, " in order ", as Hatzfeldt explained to Ampthill, " to be able to resist colonial agitation ". Ampthill's report continues : " Count Hatzfeldt then with visible embarrassment and hesitation added that the Chancellor had specially requested him to remind me that he thought himself fairly entitled to some reciprocity of good offices on the part of Her Majesty's Government in consideration of the strictly friendly attitude I knew he had maintained and flattered himself he had contributed to induce other powers to maintain in regard to the Eastern policy of Her Majesty's Government ".[2] This conversation took place on March 15. On March 19 Bleichroeder, Bismarck's private banker, visited Ferry in Paris with a " secret and personal message " from Bismarck, urging France to take up a strong line against England in Egypt. Bismarck, Bleichroeder said, was friendly, very friendly to Ferry, hoped to be even more so, and *hated* Gladstone. Ferry, not very trustful of this unofficial approach, formulated Bismarck's attitude as " I do

[1] Ampthill to Granville, No. 92, April 8, 1884. F.O. 64/1102.
[2] Ampthill to Granville, private, March, 15, 1884. G.D. 29/178. The same arguments appear in Hatzfeldt to Münster, April 4, 1884. G.P. vol. iv. No. 736, pp. 48-9.

not want to do anything to annoy England, but I should
be delighted to see her opposed by others, especially by
you ".[1] It is remarkable testimony to Bismarck's genius
that he should have at once divined the French suspicion
and, by provoking a quarrel with England, have done his
best to remove it.

The question of policy was raised for the French by the
English proposal for a conference on Egyptian affairs,
which was made to the Powers on April 23. On April 24
Bismarck and Courcel had a long conversation, beginning
with Egypt and passing on to more general topics.[2] Germany, Bismarck explained, had too slight an interest in
Egypt to take the lead in opposing England ; but his
scathing references to Gladstone (" the most useful condition to postulate for Europe's continuing her confidence
in England and allowing her to retain control of Egypt
would be the removal of a statesman so incapable as Mr.
Gladstone ") were a clear hint that France would receive
German support. Moreover, he added, Germany had her own
quarrels with England—in West Africa and in Fiji, especially in Fiji ; France, he believed, had similar colonial conflicts with England (an allusion to the Anglo-Portuguese
treaty of 1884). What was wanted was a League of Neutrals,
rather like the Armed Neutrality of 1780, to lay down the
rules to be observed in those countries not yet occupied by
a civilised power ; of course (no doubt seeing the look of
alarm on Courcel's face) their league would not need to be
armed ; that was just an illustration to make clear what he
meant. Bismarck then became reminiscent : he described
how moderate he had been towards Austria in 1866, how he
had avoided war with Russia, and how he had wanted to

[1] Note by Ferry, March 1884. D.D.F. vol. v. No. 227, pp. 242-4.

[2] Described in Courcel to Ferry, telegram, April 24, 1884. D.D.F.
vol. v. No. 246, pp. 264-5 ; private, April 25, 1884. D.D.F. vol. v. No.
247, pp. 265-6 ; dispatch, April 25, 1884. D.D.F. vol. v. No. 249, pp.
267-71.

be moderate to France in 1871—" I should not have taken Metz ; for me the deciding principle in drawing the frontier was the language ". The moral was clear—France was to make it up with Germany as Austria had done, consoling herself with the thought that, while Bismarck would not give back Alsace-Lorraine, he was sorry he had taken so much. Courcel was not deceived by the historical form of Bismarck's approach : he realised that it contained the offer of a full colonial entente against England, and he left at once for Paris to consult Ferry, not returning to Berlin until May 6.

CHAPTER II

THE ANGLO-GERMAN CONFLICT OVER ANGRA PEQUENA, APRIL–JUNE 1884

BISMARCK'S reiteration to Courcel of his Fiji grievance suggests that he had intended to pick a quarrel with England on this issue; but a little study must have convinced him that the subject was too farcical even for the establishment of an imaginary grievance.[1] West and South-West Africa provided better material. On April 19 the British government was asked to give its assistance to Dr. Nachtigal, a German colonial authority, who was going to enquire into the state of German commerce in West Africa. This area was a good deal more prosperous than the desolate wastes of South-West Africa, and there were many trading stations, both English and German. Some of the chiefs had asked to be put under British protection, but hitherto no action had been taken. When, however, in July 1884, there seemed a danger that France would attempt to seize the district as part of the French advance up the Congo, a British consul was sent to proclaim British suzerainty. To his astonishment he found that Nachtigal had bribed and bullied the chiefs into accepting German suzerainty instead. However, the French had been kept out, which was the main consideration, and the British contented themselves with pointing out that Nachtigal had secured British patronage under false pretences. But the Cameroons did not become a subject for international controversy; it is a striking illustration of the irrelevance of

[1] The Germans in Fiji claimed £150,000 as compensation; in 1885 the mixed commission, on which the British were as generous as possible, awarded them £10,000.

the colonial factor in these colonial disputes that the single German colony of any value for trading purposes was the only one acquired without difficulty.

In regard to Angra Pequena things were very different. Here there was no local action, but a determined thrusting of the question on to the international plane. On April 24, the day of Bismarck's interview with Courcel, the German consul at the Cape was instructed to announce that the Lüderitz concession was under German protection ; and a similar communication was made to the British government by Plessen, the chargé d'affaires, on April 25. This was the first Granville had heard of Angra Pequena, the previous transactions having been conducted by Pauncefote ; and Plessen knew little more than Granville. It was apparent that Bismarck was annoyed ; and Granville, being still convinced that Bismarck was opposed to colonies, supposed that Bismarck was annoyed at the English refusal to protect Angra Pequena, which had forced Bismarck to do it himself. He concluded that the way to please Bismarck was to persuade the Cape to change its mind, and he promised Plessen to find out through the Colonial Office what could be done. Thus prompted, the Colonial Office on May 7 once more raised the question with the Cape government.

Open preparations for a conflict with England were first made by Bismarck in a confidential dispatch to Münster of May 5,[1] ostensibly in reply to a remark of Granville's that he appreciated German friendship over Egypt. Germany, Bismarck wrote, wished to continue

[1] Bismarck to Münster, confidential, May 5, 1884. G.P. vol. iv. No. 738, pp. 50-52. This is the "bogy document" to which Crowe alludes in his memorandum (B.D. vol. iii. p. 415). Bismarck did not, as Crowe alleges, publish this dispatch in a White Book ; but he did assert (in a conversation with Malet, the British ambassador, on January 24, 1885) that the dispatch had threatened England with German unfriendliness unless German colonial claims were admitted, and that the dispatch had been communicated to Granville. Thimme's elaborate exculpation (*Berliner Monatsheft*, 1929) does not succeed in explaining this away.

friendly, if England also showed a friendly spirit. For instance, England should pay more attention to the German
complaints concerning the treatment of German subjects
in Fiji, and should show more consideration for German
commercial interests in Africa. Germany favoured the open
door in all parts of Africa as yet unannexed and would
recognise extensions of sovereignty only if the open door
were preserved. A further test of English intentions was
Heligoland, which was of no use to England, but which
would be very valuable to Germany ; moreover the cession
of Heligoland would have a most favourable effect on
German public opinion. " We believe that our attitude—
I will not say to England herself, as we never intend to
quarrel with her—but our attitude to the opponents or
rivals of England is more important than the possession of
Heligoland and all the commercial rivalries of German and
English firms in far distant seas." Bismarck thought the
opportunity favourable for a bargain over Heligoland ; if
Münster thought the same, he should approach Granville
at once. There was in the dispatch no mention of German
colonial claims, only the conditions on which Bismarck
would recognise the annexations of others ; and the relative
importance which Bismarck attached to the two questions,
the open door and Heligoland, was shown by his dismissing
the first in a paragraph and devoting three-quarters of the
dispatch to Heligoland.

If Bismarck emphasised Heligoland to the exclusion of
all else, he must have had good reason to do so, and the
reason is obvious. Had Bismarck at this time stated precisely to the British government that he desired colonies
and specified the areas he wanted, he would have received
his colonies and his grievance would have been at an end.
But this was the last thing Bismarck wanted : no colonial
grievance, no *rapprochement* with France. The dispatch
of May 5 was intended as a warning to the British government, but as a warning which should be incomprehensible ;

and in January 1885 Bismarck put to good use the sentence, " We shall continue to be the friends of our friends, and, without becoming enemies of England, it would not be difficult for us to be serviceable to England's permanent opponents ", quoting it as if it applied not to Heligoland, but to Germany's colonial ambitions. That Bismarck was driven to support France because of English opposition to his colonial schemes is disproved by his offer to France of an anti-English entente on April 24, before ever the Angra Pequena question had been opened or Nachtigal had sailed ; and on at least one subsequent occasion [1] Bismarck admitted that his quarrel with England had been staged with a view to his *rapprochement* with France.

But as always with Bismarck, there was in his policy an element of reinsurance ; no move was made without keeping open a line of retreat. Bismarck could not on May 5 be sure that his approach to France would have any effect (Courcel had not yet returned from Paris) ; if the French rejected his offers, he would have to continue his support of England and console himself by extracting from the English a high price for doing what he would have to do in any case. Further, if the French approach failed, he would have left on his hands a colonial quarrel with England, which he had started to impress the French ; and the colonial excitement in Germany would have to be silenced by some striking success, under cover of which the colonial difficulties could be liquidated. That striking success would be the acquisition of the " *urdeutsche* " island of Heligoland, which would be far more popular in Germany than all

[1] In a conversation with Currie on September 28, 1885. Cecil, *Life of Salisbury*, vol. iii. p. 257. Bismarck is reported to have said : " His recent attitude of unfriendliness towards England had originated in his efforts to effect a reconciliation with France and dissuade her from her obsession of revenge ". As Bismarck at that moment needed English friendship, he would of course minimise the causes of a conflict and imply (what was not the case) that the colonial conflicts would not recur.

the colonies in the world. The popularity of such a proposal was obvious, and there is no wonder that Münster, always an advocate of closer Anglo-German relations, was delighted at Bismarck's suggestion. He replied to Bismarck on May 8 that the present moment was an excellent opportunity for raising the question of Heligoland.[1] On May 11 Bismarck authorised Münster to ask for Heligoland as the price for German support of England in the Egyptian question ;[2] this authorisation is in flagrant contradiction with Bismarck's later version that, unknown to him, Münster had attached an exaggerated importance to Heligoland and none to the more serious colonial conflicts, allegedly referred to in the dispatch of May 5.

On May 17 Münster broached the topic of Heligoland to Granville, who replied—a day or two later—with some vague, conciliatory phrases about the friendship of the two countries.[3] The truth was that Granville was afraid of the Tory outcry which would follow any further surrender of territory by the Gladstone government ; but no doubt if prompted he would have become more amenable. But there was no prompting, for on May 25 Münster was abruptly ordered to drop the question of Heligoland " because of the excessive English claims concerning Angra Pequena ;"[4] and a week later there followed a long and furious dispatch, rebuking Münster for not finding in the dispatches of May 5 and May 11 what was not there.[5] This sudden change of policy was not occasioned by anything that had happened

[1] Münster to Bismarck, very confidential, May 8, 1884. G.P. vol. iv. No. 739, pp. 53-5.

[2] Bismarck to Münster, confidential, May 11, 1884. G.P. vol. iv. No. 740, pp. 55-6.

[3] Granville memorandum, May 20, 1884. G.D. 29/180. Münster's reports are referred to by Bismarck, but not published in G.P.

[4] Bismarck to Münster, telegram, May 25, 1884. G.P. vol. iv. No. 741, p. 56.

[5] Bismarck to Münster, June 1, 1884. G.P. vol. iv. No. 743, pp. 59-62.

concerning Angra Pequena. The Colonial Office was still waiting for its reply from the Cape, which it only received on May 29. It is true that Derby had stated in the House of Lords : " While we have not formally claimed the Bay, we have claimed the right to exclude Foreign Powers on the general ground of its nearness to our Settlements, and the absence of any other claims " ; [1] but this answer was given on May 19 and it is impossible to believe that Bismarck received his news from England a week late, even in the seclusion of Friedrichsruhe. Granville's answer, in similar terms, with which Bismarck made great play in his dispatch of June 1, was not made until May 27.[2]

The change in Bismarck's policy was in fact designed for France, not for England. Courcel, on his return from Paris, had an interview with Bismarck on May 12 ; Bismarck urged that the French should not engage in private negotiations with England over Egypt, but should wait for the conference, at which England would be isolated. In further conversation Bismarck, while repudiating any intention of founding colonies, had again proposed a league of neutrals—excluding England—to settle African affairs.[3] Ferry did not take Bismarck's advice ; he continued to negotiate directly with England, not without hinting that French opposition to England was being encouraged by Germany. It was the news of this French manœuvre which led Bismarck to change his policy and drop the question of Heligoland.[4] For one thing, the English were quite capable of telling the French, during their confidential negotiations,

----

[1] Hansard, cclxxxviii. col. 645.

[2] *Ibid.* p. 1450.

[3] Courcel to Ferry, telegram, May 12, 1884. D.D.F. vol. v. No. 268, pp. 286-7 ; private, May 13, 1884. No. 269, pp. 287-9 ; confidential, May 14. D.D.F. vol. v. No. 270, pp. 289-91.

[4] Hatzfeldt to Bismarck, May 24, 1884. G.P. vol. iv. No. 742, pp. 57-9. The news came from the Crown Prince, who had it from the Prince of Wales. For some unexplained reason G.P. puts this dispatch after the telegram of May 25, of which it was the cause.

of the German request for Heligoland ; this would make
the French think they had been encouraged to quarrel
with England solely to secure Heligoland for Germany, and
would therefore frighten them off the German entente
for good. On the other hand, Bismarck was undoubtedly
astute enough to have divined for himself the French attitude as expressed by Courcel in his May dispatches—
hostility to England, combined with distrust of Germany—
and it needed no great genius to foresee that the confidential
Anglo-French talks would lead to no permanent result. A
colonial conflict with England had for Bismarck a twofold
advantage : it would show the French that Germany too,
was anti-English, while its successful conclusion (which
Bismarck must have anticipated from the start) would be
a warning to the French that Bismarck could always beat
them in a competition for English friendship. The French
were hesitating—that is why Bismarck needed a short
quarrel, quickly concluded.

As so often in Bismarck's career, the behaviour of his
opponents might have been arranged for his special bene-
fit. On May 25 he decided to have a grievance about Angra
Pequena ; on May 29 the Cape government replied to
Derby that they would be responsible for the whole coast
as far as the Portuguese boundary. On June 2 Derby asked
the Foreign Office to inform the German government that
the Cape would protect Germans as well as British subjects
and that a mixed commission would be set up to decide on
claims to land. Two members of the Foreign Office thought
this a rather inadequate answer to Münster's query as to
title, but Pauncefote endorsed it in a minute, which, while
perhaps a little peremptory, shows that the British government were acting in all good faith.[1] The communication was

---

[1] Pauncefote's minute reads: "I see no objection. The German Government have asked what rights we claim over the territory in question—
as they do not at present recognise our sovereignty and must therefore
protect the German subjects settled there. The Colonial Office now

not however made, as on June 3 the news of the Cape's intention to extend its sovereignty reached Berlin, and on June 4 Münster was instructed to say that the German government could not recognise the Cape's action. The British government was taken completely by surprise ; it still failed to discover whether Germany claimed sovereignty over Angra Pequena—Derby thought it did,[1] Pauncefote that it did not [2]—and as Bismarck himself, as late as June 8, did not know whether he was pursuing a colonial policy the British doubt is understandable.[3] Granville,

proposes to reply that H.M. Govt. have decided to annex the territory as part of the British Dominions and to exercise the rights of Sovty. thereover and consequently to extend British protection to all persons residing therein."

[1] A telegram from Hatzfeldt, communicated by Münster on June 6, that Germany could not recognise the right of the Cape to annex Angra Pequena is minuted :

" This seems to mean that the German government intends to lay claim to Angra Pequena as German territory.

" Of course they do not mean to include Walfisch Bay, which we have held since 1877 or 78—they not objecting.

" We must abstain from taking any action on the recommendation of the Cape colony till the question of right is settled.

" How is this to be done ? By arbitration ?

" Our claim may not be a strong one, I do not think it is : but I cannot conceive what claim the Germans have to put forward.

" D[erby], June 8."

[2] Ampthill to Granville, No. 145, June 7, 1884. F.O. 64/1102 reports a meeting of the Colonial Society in Berlin. This is minuted : "It seems to be a question now what the German Government meant by intimating that Angra Pequena had been placed under the protection of the Empire. Do they intend to claim Sovereignty over the place ?—G. D[allas]."

" I think not. Their language has been that as we do not claim sovereignty German subjects are entitled to German protection. But they may lately have some scheme of a German Protectorate there —J. P[auncefote]."

[3] Münster's dispatch of June 7 reported Granville as saying he had never received the impression that " the German government wanted to pursue a colonial policy ". This Bismarck minuted : " What is colonial policy ? We must protect our fellow-countrymen." G.P. vol. iv. p.64

quite bewildered by the whole affair, told Münster that there must have been some misunderstanding and hoped that nothing would be done before the two governments had reached an agreement.[1] The decision to annex was not proceeded with, and the matter was left to be discussed with Herbert Bismarck, who was due in London the following week. There was thus no attempt to forestall German plans ; Bismarck was not in any way " thwarted " ; and the confusion which existed was due entirely to the failure of the German government to formulate its intentions clearly.

However, the affair served its purpose : it provided Bismarck with a quarrel which should show the French that he had real grievances against England and was not trying to do a deal with the English at their expense. But the rapid termination of the quarrel was to show the French also that Germany could return to good relations if she chose. The Anglo-French negotiations over the Egyptian conference continued to progress and agreement was reached on June 16. It was only to be expected that Bismarck too should display a renewed desire to be on the best of terms with England and that the dispute between them should now appear as trifling as before it had been grave. On June 9 Bismarck spoke to Ampthill for the first time about Angra Pequena : the British delays would, he feared, cause a lasting resentment in Germany—" his own feelings of friendship towards England could never change—but the national feeling of Germany would, he anticipated, become less cordial than heretofore and would seek to influence his foreign policy." [2] Bismarck did not even now say outright that Germany wanted colonies ; his complaint was merely of delays, which could have been obviated by either Bis-

[1] Granville to Ampthill, confidential, No. 161A, June 7, 1884. F.O. 64/1102 ; Münster to Bismarck, June 7, 1884. G.P. vol. iv. No. 744, pp. 63-4.

[2] Ampthill to Granville, private, June 14, 1884. G.D. 29/178.

marck or Hatzfeldt speaking to Ampthill at any time within the previous six months.

The question was at last discussed at three conversations between Granville and Herbert Bismarck—on June 14, June 17, and June 21 ; [1] and, despite the fact that Granville was suffering from gout and that Herbert Bismarck regarded it as his duty to be persistently rude, agreement was reached without any difficulty. Granville again apologised for his failure to understand the German position, and, armed with a memorandum from Herbert Bismarck which purported to recapitulate the negotiations, he had no difficulty in persuading the Cabinet to agree to the German claims. Granville pointed out to Herbert Bismarck that he was not making any sort of bargain—" each question ought to be discussed on its merits "—and that he counted on German support not because of colonial bribes but " because of the general policy which during the four years I had been in office His Highness had consistently and successfully pursued with a view to maintaining the peace of Europe ". At the final interview on June 21, after the Cabinet meeting, it was agreed between them that their understanding should be recorded in a dispatch from Granville to Ampthill, and Granville then ran over the main lines of it with Herbert : Germany " had no intention to establish State Colonies, but merely to give protection to her subjects " ; this claim the British government would recognise as soon as Germany agreed to the establishment of a mixed commission (on the analogy of Fiji !) to examine private British claims to land in the area and as soon as Germany confirmed Herbert Bismarck's statement that they had no intention of establishing Penal Settlements. The area covered by the German claim was not, even now,

[1] Granville to Ampthill, No. 169A, 169B, June 14, 1884 ; confidential, No. 178, June 18, 1884 ; confidential, No. 180, June 21, 1884. F.O. 64/1102 ; Herbert Bismarck to Bismarck, June 16, June 17, June 22. G.P. vol. iv. No. 745, 746, 747, pp. 64-74.

distinctly stated : both sides assumed that they were talking
about the Lüderitz concession—itself a vague enough area.
At first it was described as 150 square miles but subsequently swelled to 3000—and there was never at this
time any suggestion that Germany (on no ground but appe-
tite) claimed everything between the Orange River and
the Portuguese boundary. One passing remark of Herbert
Bismarck's remains to be quoted : after saying that it was
no concern of England's whether some power actually proclaimed sovereignty over territory which the British government had admitted did not belong to them, he added
[English in the original], " none of the other powers for
instance would care if you proclaimed the Queen's sovereignty over North Borneo or New Guinea ".

These negotiations with Herbert Bismarck had of
course a rather irregular character : Münster, the ordinary
channel of communication, was never consulted at all, apparently not even informed of what had taken place, and
Herbert Bismarck had not even a subordinate position at
the London embassy, having just been appointed minister
at the Hague. But he recorded the conversations in official
(though unnumbered) dispatches, not in private letters,
and his remarks were as binding as those of any other
official German representative. For the moment the results
of Herbert Bismarck's visit were all that could have been
wished. Granville felt that an unfortunate misunderstanding had been cleared up by the well-tried Whig method of
personal relations ; Bismarck expressed his gratitude to
Ampthill for the *final* settlement of the Angra Pequena
question, and Ampthill, still confident in Bismarck's
friendship for England and for himself, surmised that the
affair had been thrust upon Bismarck against his will ; [1]

[1] Ampthill to Granville, private, June 28, 1884. G.D. 29/178.
Ampthill's letters nowhere record an actual statement by Bismarck that
his hand had been forced, as Sanderson implies in his minutes of 1907,
B.D. vol. iii. p. 422.

and Courcel immediately noted that the German press
—and Bismarck's own public utterances—had become
" very polite towards the English and, to say the least,
cold towards France ".[1] Meanwhile in England the Foreign
Office and the Colonial Office were left with the task of
trying to discover exactly what had been agreed upon between Granville and Herbert Bismarck,[2] and it was not
until July 14 that the dispatch to Ampthill,[3] embodying
the agreement, was sent off. At the same time the Cape
government, who were still waiting for an answer to their

[1] Courcel to Ferry, telegram, June 25, 1884. D.D.F. vol. v. No. 322,
p. 338.

[2] The following gives some idea of the confusion (F.O. 64/1102) :
R. Herbert [Colonial Office] to Pauncefote, early July :

" I believe the Cab. has generally approved the record made by Lord
Granville, after consulting Lord Derby and Lord Kimberley, that the
history of past transactions precludes this Country from claiming the
sovereignty or the protection of the Coast between the Orange River
and latitude 18°, and obliges us to agree to a compromise by which the
German Govt. shall either (a) jointly with us protect that Coast, or (b)
protect its subjects on that Coast and leave to us the right and duty of
protecting ours ; both Governments declaring that they will not exercise sovereignty (a) either on any part of that Coast or (b) on any part
of the Coast within which subjects of the other power now have concessions capable of being verified ; and that neither power shall send
convicts to any place on that Coast."

This is minuted : " Lord G. I understood you have settled the pre-
liminaries with Count Herbert Bismarck. Shall we now communicate
the result to the C.O. and ask them to indicate the course they now
propose we should take as to an enquiry, etc.—J. P[auncefote], July 7."

" Did I not ask that a draft should be prepared on the lines of my
answer in the Lords [June 30. Hansard, cclxxxix. col. 1654] and proposing a Commission.—G[ranville]."

The Colonial Office draft of July 8 is minuted by Granville : " Is it
necessary to define so much the territory to be protected by Germany ?

" We have no agreement yet with the Germans as to its being confined to the concession of M. Lüderitz.

" Rather large words not committing ourselves one way or the other
would be better."

[3] Granville to Ampthill, No. 200, July 14, 1884. F.O. 64/1102.

proposal of May 29, were told that Great Britain could not oppose a German Protectorate where German subjects had acquired concessions, but that the way was now open for the Cape to annex the rest of the coast as far as the Portuguese boundary. This the Cape resolved to do on July 16 ; the news of the Cape intention was published in *The Times*, and the proposal of the British government to place the coast, except round Angra Pequena, under the control of the Cape was announced in the House of Commons on July 29.[1]

[1] Hansard, vol. ccxci. col. 851.

CHAPTER III

ANGRA PEQUENA GROWS INTO GERMAN
SOUTH-WEST AFRICA, JULY–SEPTEMBER 1884

THE finality of the settlement of the Angra Pequena question was, however, dependent on the finality of the agreement between England and France, which rendered an Anglo-German quarrel both unnecessary and unwelcome ; and the agreement between England and France was by no means final, for the London conference, instead of settling the Egyptian question, produced a new and more irreconcilable conflict. The conference met on June 28 ; it began to get into difficulties on July 12; on July 28 it came to an open disagreement between the English and French representatives, the other powers abstaining ; on August 2 the conference broke up without result. The French were told that Münster had been instructed to support the French demands ; [1] but in fact Münster made his vote conditional on Russian co-operation, which was not forthcoming, and the French were left alone. On August 12, that is after the breakdown of the conference, Bismarck rebuked Münster for his failure to express the German position and support France ; [2] but as Bismarck does not refer to any previous instructions, and as none are printed in the *Grosse Politik*, this seems to be another instance of Münster not finding in his instructions what was not there. [3]

[1] Ferry to Waddington, telegram, July 27, 1884. D.D.F. vol. v. No. 345, p. 354.

[2] Bismarck to Münster, Aug. 12, 1884. G.P. vol. iv. No 749, pp. 77-8.

[3] It may be objected that Münster would have defended himself against such baseless charges ; but Münster must have known that Bismarck was anxious to get rid of him—it was common talk at the

It is more than probable that Bismarck, foreseeing the breakdown of the conference, had been not unwilling to see France forced into open and isolated opposition to England and the way thus barred against a repetition of the French manœuvre of May.[1]

The renewed quarrel between England and France was accompanied at each stage by a revival of the Angra Pequena question. So long as the conference was still in being, the disputes were over points of detail. Ampthill delivered the Angra Pequena Note to the Germans on July 19 : on July 22 the German government—through the first secretary at London—asked for the deletion of the phrase that Germany " had no intention to establish state colonies ".[2] This may well have been for purely domestic considerations, as the Note would ultimately be made public and such a phrase would produce an outcry from the colonial party ; but the objection to the phrase that Germany would not establish Penal Settlements, which was expressed by Hatzfeldt on July 24 [3] and by Münster in an official Note on July 29, is difficult to explain on any ground other than the desire to renew a quarrel. As Pauncefote pointed out : " The friendly settlement of this question was arranged at private interviews between Lord Granville and Herbert Bismarck and the form of Dispatch to Lord Ampthill was settled by them in conversation on the subject. It is somewhat inconsistent with the spirit of the negotiations that an official Dispatch should be written by the German Government objecting to the terms of the Note of Lord Ampthill. They might have privately sug-

time—and an attempt to contradict Bismarck would have given the latter just the evidence of insubordination he needed to persuade the aged William I. to dismiss one of his oldest and most loyal servants.

[1] Courcel suspected that Münster's action was not so unwelcome to Bismarck as he made out to the French. Courcel to Ferry, private, Sept. 15, 1884. D.D.F. vol. v. No. 399, p. 410.

[2] Minute by Pauncefote, July 22, 1884. F.O. 64/1102.

[3] Ampthill to Granville, No. 207, July 25, 1884.

gested any modification of form."[1] However, Granville with-
drew the objectionable phrases without demur on August 7.[2]

The breakdown of the Egyptian conference was Bismarck's cue for a new approach to France, and this was of
course accompanied by renewed and public conflict with
England on colonial topics. Ampthill was " in perfect
despair " at Bismarck's anti-English attitude, which he
regarded as an electioneering device to increase Bismarck's
popularity,[3] and he did not conceal his discouragement
from Courcel.[4] On August 7 Bismarck wrote to Hatzfeldt
that the present moment after the breakdown of the London conference was particularly suitable for proposing to
France measures for securing the open door in all parts
of Africa as yet unannexed ; France and Germany, when
they had reached an agreement, could then invite the
other colonial powers to adhere to it ; England, because
of her ambition to monopolise the whole world outside
Europe, would probably refuse and would have to be
faced with an association of the other states, similar to
the Armed Neutrality of the eighteenth century.[5] Acting
on these instructions, Hatzfeldt approached Courcel, and
at a series of interviews—on August 11,[6] 13,[7] 14,[8]

[1] Granville to Ampthill, No. 217, July 29, and Pauncefote minute,
July 31, 1884. F.O. 64/1102.

[2] Granville to Ampthill, No. 225B, Aug. 7, 1884. F.O. 64/1103.

[3] Ampthill to Granville, private, Aug. 2, 1884. G.D. 29/178.

[4] Courcel to Ferry, private, Aug. 9, 1884. D.D.F. vol. v. No. 357,
p. 362.

[5] Bismarck to Hatzfeldt, Aug. 7, 1884. G.P. vol. iii. No. 680, pp.
413-14.

[6] Hatzfeldt to Bismarck, Aug. 11, 1884. G.P. vol. iii. No. 681, pp.
414-17 ; Courcel to Ferry, telegram, Aug. 11. D.D.F. vol. v. No. 361,
p. 365.

[7] Hatzfeldt to Bismarck, Aug. 13. G.P. vol. iii. No. 682, p. 418 ;
Courcel to Ferry, telegram, August 14, 1884. D.D.F. vol. v. No. 365, pp.
367-8.

[8] Courcel to Ferry, telegram, Aug. 15, 1884. D.D.F. vol. v. No. 366;
pp. 368-9.

16,[1] and 17 [2]—proposals for a colonial agreement were worked out in detail. Hatzfeldt made no secret of the fact that the plan was directed against England, and argued that, as it committed Germany to opposing England in colonial matters, it would guarantee German support for France in the Egyptian question (Münster's unfortunate conduct was of course explained away). Courcel, as his reports show, was very pleased with the German proposals; Ferry, perhaps from distrust of Bismarck or from fear of French public opinion, was more hesitant and gave Hohenlohe an evasive answer, when approached by him on August 15. But that his answer was not a refusal was shown by his summoning Courcel to Paris for a thorough examination of the German proposals.[3] Courcel arrived in Paris on August 18.

Courcel's visit to Paris coincided most accurately with a renewed hostility between England and Germany. There had been no secret about the British intention to annex the South-West African coast outside the Lüderitz concession ; and the British government, having made the decision, left the Cape to take the practical steps at its leisure. On August 16 Plessen, the German chargé d'affaires, called at the Foreign Office to say that the coast line from the Orange river [the Cape boundary] to latitude 26° [Angra Pequena] was under German protection, and on the 18th he came again to protest against any annexations by the Cape in this area. On August 22 he paid another visit to say that, as England had in 1880 declared that the Orange river was the limit of her authority, Germany

[1] Courcel to Ferry, telegram, Aug. 16, 1884. D.D.F. vol. v. No. 369, pp. 371-2.

[2] Bismarck to Hatzfeldt, Aug. 15, 1884. G.P. vol. iii. No. 683, pp. 418-19 ; Hatzfeldt to Bismarck, Aug. 17, 1884. G.P. vol. iii. No. 685, p. 420 ; Courcel to Ferry, telegram, Aug. 17, 1884, No. 372, pp. 373-5.

[3] Hohenlohe to Bismarck, Aug. 15, 1884. G.P. vol. iii. No. 684, pp. 419-20.

would object to any extension of British sovereignty at this moment ; finally on August 26 he announced that German protection extended as far north as latitude 18° [the Portuguese boundary]. The German claim was thus carried beyond Walfish Bay and received an addition of six hundred miles of coast line in a single week. Meanwhile an announcement of the hoisting of the German flag had been issued by the German consul at Cape Town on August 22. Granville was quite bewildered by the renewal of German hostility, as recorded by Ampthill [1] and as manifested at the London conference. His friendly talks with Herbert Bismarck had, he believed, removed all the German colonial grievances, and, running over the negotiations of the past few months, he could only suppose that Bismarck was annoyed because Granville had not replied more definitely to Münster's proposal for the cession of Heligoland. He therefore proposed to write to Herbert Bismarck, asking whether Germany had any grievance ; this would give Bismarck an opportunity to renew the demand for Heligoland if that was what he wanted. Both Derby and Gladstone had doubts as to the wisdom of these unofficial negotiations,[2]

---

[1] Ampthill's last letter (he died suddenly on August 24) to Granville, Aug. 16, G.D. 29/178, described the newspaper campaign against England as " too stupid ".

[2] Gladstone to Granville, Aug. 19, 1884. G.D. 29/128 :

" I can take no exception whatever to your proposed letter to Bismarck though I imagine that a very captious critic might not like your approaching one, with whom you deal on equal terms, through his son."

Derby to Granville, Aug. 20, 1884. G.D. 29/120 :

" I see nothing *infra dig.* in asking indirectly what is Bismarck's grievance. It is clear that he either has one, or thinks fit to pretend that he has. In either case we have a right to know what it is, or what he means us to think it is. But are you quite prudent in passing over Münster and working through young Bismarck ? You know best, but M. is half English and thoroughly friendly, and we know little of Bismarck.—If Münster learns what is passing you will make an enemy of him. Is it worth while ?

" If Bismarck wants Heligoland he is taking the wrong way to get

and even Granville was not very hopeful.[1] However, on August 20 he sent off a letter to Herbert Bismarck, in which he appealed to their friendly relations in the past and, after pointing out that all the colonial difficulties had been settled in Germany's favour, asked him " whether there is any matter of discussion between the two Governments on which a misunderstanding may exist and which might easily be cleared up ".[2]

Herbert Bismarck must have received this letter almost at the very moment when Courcel returned from Paris. Courcel had persuaded Ferry to welcome the German offer of an entente ; but the proposals were made more definite, and, in particular, emphasis on preserving the open door in central Africa changed an anti-English demonstration (" *une machine de guerre contre l'Angleterre* ", as Ferry described it) into a programme which England with her Free Trade enthusiasm would herself welcome.[3] In a conversation with Hatzfeldt on August 25 Courcel explained that, for the sake of French public opinion, any co-operation between France and Germany should direct itself to concrete issues ; in any case the attempt to lay down general principles to cover the whole of Africa would lead to innumerable disputes, and they would do better to concentrate on the Congo area, where the activities of the International Association raised practical questions ; he further made it

it. We might cede it for a consideration (it is really no use to us) but we cannot be bullied out of it."

[1] Granville to Ampthill, Aug. 21, 1884. G.D. 29/178 :

" I doubt it's doing good, but I do not see that it can do harm. . . .

" This country can afford to be isolated for a time, but the having Egypt on our hands makes a very great difference.

" . . . Münster seemed to think that the German F.O. is more hostile than the Chancellor."

[2] Granville to Herbert Bismarck, confidential, Aug. 20, 1884. G.D. 29/207 ; G.P. vol. iv. 751, pp. 79-80.

[3] Note by Ferry on the German proposals, Aug. 1884. D.D.F. vol. v. No. 376, pp. 377 80.

clear that France was not prepared to oppose England on the Egyptian question alone, but would act only so far as she was supported by the other powers.[1] This conversation was followed by an invitation for Courcel to visit Bismarck at Varzin, from August 26 to 28. The conversation of the 26th turned on Egypt, and Bismarck did not conceal his disappointment at the reserved attitude of the French. The discussion on Africa, of August 27, went much better—the two governments were to agree on the general principles governing effective occupation and the open door in West Africa and would then invite the other colonial powers to a conference. Bismarck had taken full notice of Courcel's remark to Hatzfeldt about limiting the co-operation between the two countries to concrete issues, and during the whole visit he made but one fleeting reference to the idea of a general entente.[2] But his expressions of goodwill towards the French activities in China and the emphatic promise that no German attempts at annexations in Africa would be countenanced where they clashed with French claims were indication enough of the general policy he was pursuing; and proof too, if that were needed, that his quarrels with England were part of a general policy, not isolated misunderstandings.

After the progress made with Courcel there could of course be no question of replying seriously to Granville's letter of August 20. On August 30 Herbert Bismarck, on Bismarck's instructions, sent off to Granville a long letter full of platitudes. " The strong language of the newspapers and the complaints of the German Government . . . have no

[1] Courcel to Ferry, telegram, Aug. 25, 1884. D.D.F. vol. v. No. 377, pp. 381-3 ; Hatzfeldt to Bismarck, Aug. 25, 1884. G.P. vol. iii. No. 687, pp. 421-4.

[2] Courcel to Ferry, confidential, Aug. 30. 1884. D.D.F. vol. v. No. 385, pp. 390-5 ; Bismarck to Busch, Aug. 30, 1884. G.P. vol. iii. No. 688, pp. 424-6. Bismarck places both conversations on August 27, but Courcel's account, which is fuller, says the first took place on the evening of his arrival.

other meaning but to prove the strong desire of the German people and the German Government to maintain the actual good relations with England." And again : " If there exists some irritation in Germany it has merely been caused by the Colonial Office and not by the Foreign Office : such feeling therefore hardly will be strong enough to change friendly policy ". The Bismarcks, father and son, were particularly proud of this sentence : " I remember having heard my father say that on the whole the best plan to maintain and strengthen existing good relations between the two countries was to treat each other in a gentleman-like way, and I am sure that you thoroughly agree with him ". The only practical statement in the letter was the hope that the British government would not support the annexations proposed by the Cape in South-West Africa.[1] Less than a week after writing this letter Herbert Bismarck was listening with approval to the remarks of a French diplomat (Barrère, the French representative in Cairo) that the *rapprochement* between France and Germany was " not only the best for both countries, but for the whole world and for world progress. They must bear in mind later generations and the fact that the strongest alliance in the world would be the Franco-German : once that was established, no one else would be able to say a word." [2]

Bismarck may not have shared Barrère's enthusiasm, but he was hard at work consolidating the Franco-German entente. Bismarck's position was strengthened at this moment by the meeting of the three Emperors at Skiernie-wice, which took place from September 15 to 17, and which —by reaffirming the friendship between Russia and Austria at any rate temporarily—secured Bismarck against either Russian hostility to Austria or Russian temptations to

[1] Herbert Bismarck to Granville, Aug. 30, 1884. G.D. 29/180 ; G.P. vol. iv. No. 752, pp. 81-3.

[2] Memorandum by Herbert Bismarck, Sept. 7, 1884. G.P. vol. iii. No. 689, p. 427.

France. Bismarck took great pains to emphasise to Courcel
that this manifestation of the League of the Three Emperors was in no way directed against France and that it
did not involve French isolation. The only practical question to be discussed at Skierniewice, he told Courcel before
the meeting took place,[1] would be the extradition of political
criminals; a slight and significant because very unusual
courtesy was that the Note of September 13, relating to the
West African proposals, was written in French and signed
by Bismarck (instead of Hatzfeldt);[2] and Bismarck, on
his return to Berlin, came to see Courcel at the French
embassy, thus breaking a long-standing rule of his against
paying calls in Berlin. At this visit of September 21 Bismarck was in great spirits; he had evidently forgotten,
or had decided to ignore, Courcel's reluctance to discuss
generalities. He began by explaining away the meeting at
Skierniewice, but he soon passed on to abuse Münster for
his failure to oppose England strongly enough at the London Conference. Herbert, Bismarck continued, was about
to visit England, but Bismarck had told him to refuse to
see Lord Granville; moreover Herbert had, at his advice,
written to Granville " that we thought affairs between
friendly Cabinets should be treated as between *gentlemen*
and that the conduct of England did not appear to have
conformed to this rule." [3] This led Bismarck on to a general
denunciation of English colonial policy; what was needed
was a league of all the secondary maritime powers, led by
France—after all, both Napoleon I. and Napoleon III. had
had the same idea; it was in the tradition of French policy.[4]

[1] Courcel to Ferry, telegram, Sept. 12, 1884. D.D.F. vol. v. No. 394,
pp. 403-4.

[2] Courcel to Billot (Directeur des Affaires politiques), Sept. 15,
1884. D.D.F. vol. v. No. 400, pp. 413-14.

[3] Courcel to Ferry, confidential, Sept. 21, 1884. D.D.F. vol. v. No.
405, pp. 418-22.

[4] Courcel to Ferry, confidential, Sept. 23, 1884. D.D.F. vol. v. No.
407, pp. 423-5 (a further extract is in Bourgeois and Pages, *Origines de*

Bismarck was thus renewing the approach to France which he had first tried without much success in April. Even now Courcel was hesitant ; but the colonial quarrel with England had had the desired effect—it had convinced Courcel, if not Ferry, that Bismarck's hostility to England was genuine and likely to be permanent.[1] He wrote to Ferry on September 28 : " The industrial development of Germany . . . is driving her to colonial ventures and there she will inevitably meet the ruthless rivalry of England. The antagonism between the two powers—industrial, colonial, and maritime antagonism—should, it seems to me, be permanent." [2] Courcel felt that he could take a month's holiday without this time running the risk of finding Bismarck pro-English on his return.

While Bismarck had been denouncing to Courcel the extravagant colonial claims of England, the English had been engaged in a final surrender to Germany concerning South-West Africa. The dispatch, recognising the German claim to the entire coast from the Orange river to the Portuguese boundary, was sent to Berlin on September 19 [3] and communicated to the German government on September 24 ; it received from Bismarck the cool reply : " Prince Bismarck sees in that communication a first step in the direction which he had hoped British Policy would take.—He could have wished in the interests of the present

la grande Guerre, p. 385). The conversation continues the topics discussed in the previous reference, but seems to have taken place later in the day. Cf. Courcel to Ferry, telegram, Sept. 21, 1884. D.D.F. vol. v. No. 404, p. 417-18.

[1] The German hostility to England was also shown in renewed support to France over the Egyptian question, which had entered a new stage on September 18 when England claimed to dispose of the surplus Caisse de la Dette.

[2] Courcel to Ferry, private, Sept. 28, 1884. D.D.F. vol. v. No. 410, pp. 427-9.

[3] Granville to Scott, chargé d'affaires, Sept. 19, 1884. F.O. 64/1103.

and the future that it had been taken earlier." [1] With this interchange the Angra Pequena question was closed ; even Bismarck could not squeeze any further disputes out of it. There was some discussion about the islands off the coast which had been in effective and undisputed British occupation for many years ; even these the British government was willing, despite the reluctance of the Colonial Office, to surrender for a nominal concession.[2] The question was not, however, followed up ; Bismarck was not prepared to pay anything for the islands and he could hardly make a grievance out of the British refusal to surrender British territory for nothing.

All the German demands had thus been met without resistance, though with some delay. The Colonial Office was indeed very much to blame for its dilatoriness, which annoyed Bismarck without deterring him ; but its slowness was no more culpable than Bismarck's failure to formulate his demands clearly. No serious defence of the German claims was ever advanced : there was no " effective occupation " such as Bismarck demanded of others, and the Lüderitz concession itself was extracted from the natives by the most dubious means. Moreover, despite Bismarck's strictures on British acquisitiveness, the British frontier in South-West Africa was not advanced an inch. Germany took all she wanted : Great Britain took nothing. There was no particular virtue in this : the Colonial Office had contemplated extending British suzerainty only because of colonial agitation and because of what it thought were the promptings of Bismarck. No one in the Colonial Office can have been under any delusion as to the value of the territory, and the Germans soon discovered (what Bismarck

---

[1] Minute by Lister of a conversation with the German chargé d'affaires, Sept. 27, 1884. F.O. 64/1103.

[2] Granville to Malet, No. 374A, Nov. 28, 1884. F.O. 64/1104. The original (rather intransigent) Colonial Office draft was considerably toned down by Gladstone.

no doubt knew all along) that South-West Africa was no Eldorado. In 1889 Herbert Bismarck, now Secretary of State, paid a visit to England and contemplated surrendering German South-West Africa in exchange for Heligoland. Two passages from his letters provide a curious postscript to the dispute of 1884. He wrote to his father on March 27, 1889 : [1] " I think the deal would be very advantageous for us and enormously popular in Germany. Our South-West African Company is stagnant, bankrupt, and hopeless. We are in a mess with our Commissioner, who has had to flee to the English Walfisch Bay, and in the colonial area we have not in fact a single soul who would qualify as a German citizen [*reichsangehörig*]." And on June 21, 1889, Herbert Bismarck wrote a dispatch to the Under-Secretary which concluded : [2] " If we keep South-West Africa, we shall be compelled to spend more than hitherto on police, protection, and administration, and for the time being there is no prospect of trade and capital following our flag. Complaints that we did wrong to surrender these colonies will start only when, after the exchange, the English and Cape colonists develop the mines, pastures, etc., and make a good thing out of it."

[1] Herbert Bismarck to Bismarck, private, March 27, 1889. G.P. vol. iv. No. 946, p. 409.

[2] Herbert Bismarck to Berchem, June 21, 1889. G.P. vol. iv. No. 952, pp. 416-17.

CHAPTER IV

AN INTERVAL OF RESERVE, OCTOBER–DECEMBER 1884

TOWARDS the end of September 1884, Herbert Bismarck paid a private visit to England. Acting on his father's instructions he avoided seeing Granville, giving as his excuse that Granville had not answered his letter of August 30 : he did not, however, inform the British politicians to whom he made this complaint that his letter had been in answer to one from Granville. When the complaint reached Granville's ears, he wrote to Herbert Bismarck on October 2, explaining that he had not answered because he had thought " the proper rejoinder was to meet the Chancellor's wishes concerning Angra Pequena ; " [1] to this letter Herbert did not reply—nor is it referred to in the *Grosse Politik*. Herbert Bismarck's task in England was clearly to display the German sense of grievance, without specifying any grievance too precisely, for fear it might be redressed. He had conversations with a number of Cabinet ministers (Chamberlain, Dilke, and Hartington); he also dilated on the German grievances to the Prince of Wales and, at the Prince's request, to Ponsonby, the Queen's private secretary.[2] He gave them all a highly coloured version of the Angra Pequena affair and suggested that Granville was deliberately suppressing his letter of August 30. On the whole, Herbert Bismarck overdid it : the simultaneous British surrender, unknown to Herbert Bismarck, on every point at

[1] Granville to Herbert Bismarck, private, Oct. 2, 1884. G.D. 29/207.
[2] Memorandum by Herbert Bismarck, Sept. 24, 1884. G.P. vol. iv. No. 753 ; Herbert Bismarck to Bismarck, Oct. 1, 1884. G.P. vol. iv. No. 754 ; Memorandum by Herbert Bismarck, October 5, 1884. G.P. vol. iv. No. 755, pp. 83-91.

issue, made his tale of grievance rather empty, and when
Granville—in answer to Herbert's insinuations—circulated
their correspondence the members of the Cabinet felt
that Granville came rather well out of the affair. Chamberlain, the most pro-German member of the Cabinet, wrote :
" Bismarck's letter is not so frank or so clear as he described it. . . . He does not explain what was the precise
thing he wants of us. . . . He did not tell me that his letter
was in answer to one from Lord Granville—who seems to
have done all in his power to conciliate him." Derby's
minute was, naturally, even cooler : " Either Germans are
the most irritable of mortals (which I do not think them)
or there is something behind. I have always suspected
disappointment on the part of Bismarck at not having succeeded in making us quarrel with France." [1]

Herbert Bismarck, after his stay in England, proceeded
to Paris, where he had a long interview with Ferry and
several conversations with Courcel, who was home on leave.
Ferry still harboured the suspicion that Bismarck wanted to
weaken France by forcing her into a conflict with England,
and Herbert received urgent instructions from Bismarck
to assure Ferry that Germany wanted a peaceful solution
of the Egyptian question and would deplore a war between
France and England as much as one between Russia and
Austria.[2] Herbert, who prided himself on his knowledge
of English politics, had convinced himself that a Tory
government was out of the question; he was therefore able
to assure Ferry, who knew perfectly well that Gladstone
was the only English minister to take the English promise
to evacuate Egypt seriously, that Bismarck did not desire
the overthrow of the Gladstone ministry. For one thing,
he said, Bismarck had promised Russia not to attack

[1] Minutes on the correspondence with Herbert Bismarck, circulated
by Granville, Oct. 1884. G.D. 29/144.
[2] Bismarck to Herbert Bismarck, telegram, Oct. 5 and 6, 1884.
G.P. vol. iii. No. 693, p. 431.

Gladstone—who was obviously more friendly to Russia than any alternative Prime Minister; and further Bismarck regarded the Gladstone Cabinet as *the worst Ministry for England and therefore the best for everyone else.* Herbert Bismarck was very pleased with the effect of his remarks on Ferry, but in fact Ferry was still doubtful; he still suspected that Germany would let him down and he wrote in his note of the interview : " His [Bismarck's] manifest tendency is to push us forward, promising to follow us; our policy is to wait and not to take any step without the support of Europe ".[1]

The general policy, which Bismarck had pursued from the beginning of August until early October, had been irritation with, and hostility towards, England, coupled with friendship towards France, which produced ever-increasing offers of co-operation and support. Soon after Herbert's interview with Ferry this policy was reversed : there was renewed friendship with England and renewed hostility, at or any rate coldness, towards France. It is only possible to guess at the reasons for this change, for there are no documents in the *Grosse Politik* for the period between October 7 and December 5, by which date the direction of Bismarck's policy was changing once more. Bismarck may have been a little mollified by the English surrender over South-West Africa ; though the entire question was too trivial to have much influence on his general policy. On the other hand, Bismarck, reading between the lines of Herbert's interview with Ferry, may well have deduced Ferry's hesitation and have decided to try the effect of a little coldness ; or Bismarck, a man who liked quick results, may have been genuinely impatient at the French reserve. In January 1885, Bismarck put all the blame on

[1] Herbert Bismarck to Bismarck, Oct. 6, 1884. G.P. vol. iii. No. 694 ; Oct. 7, 1884. G.P. vol. iii. No. 695, pp. 431-9 ; note by Ferry of conversation with Herbert Bismarck, Oct. 6, 1884 D.D.F. vol. v. No. 421, pp. 441-3.

Courcel ; [1] Courcel, he said, had found that he had gone further to meet Germany than his government approved, and had told Bismarck on his return that he would have to be more reserved. It is perfectly true that Courcel was keener than Ferry on the *rapprochement* with Germany (though not so unreservedly as Bismarck thought), and he may well have expressed to Bismarck a disappointment which, naturally, he did not report to Ferry ; but this is certainly not the whole explanation, for the change in Bismarck's policy had taken place before ever he saw Courcel on his return. Both factors—the English concessions and the French reserve—may have played a part in influencing Bismarck; but a display of coldness after an approach was too regular a tactic of Bismarck's to need any concrete explanation, and later events show that he was still pursuing the same object of wooing the French, though by a different method.

Sir Edward Malet, the new British ambassador at Berlin, took up his post in the middle of October and had a very friendly interview with Bismarck on his arrival. Bismarck spoke warmly of Granville's desire to meet German wishes, and put all the blame for the late quarrel on the selfish and short-sighted attitude of Derby. Malet, who was a capable and experienced observer, doubted the sincerity of the past colonial fuss. "His manner", he wrote of Bismarck, " was eminently friendly and cordial and gave me the impression that what I may be allowed to call his past ill-humour has been rather the result of political calculation than personal sentiment."[2] Courcel, on his return to Berlin early in November, was at once made to feel the change

---

[1] Bismarck to Hohenlohe, Jan. 24, 1885. G.P. vol. iii. No. 697, pp. 440-41.

[2] Malet to Granville, No. 331, confidential, Oct. 23, 1884. F.O. 64/1104. In the dispatch Malet referred only to Bismarck's attacks on the Colonial Office, but in a private letter to Granville, Oct. 24 (G.D. 29/179) added that Bismarck attacked Derby by name.

in Bismarck's attitude. In a conversation on November 12 Bismarck expressed his dissatisfaction with France : he was, he said, very hurt that France (who was engaged in a dispute with China) should have even considered English mediation, whereas German mediation had been ruled out as impossible. Bismarck, on his side, now refused to support France in the Egyptian question—" If he had found France ready to forget the past and pursue frankly a policy of interests, he would have been ready to support her, but he could not risk quarrelling with England in view of the mood in which France remained. He repeated that he was not annoyed but discouraged." [1] As Ferry at once replied to Courcel, French policy had not changed in the slightest since the halcyon days of September ; [2] but perhaps the offence lay in this continued adherence to the policy of co-operation on concrete issues. Courcel, suffering a little from a guilty conscience, found it difficult to explain Bismarck's change to Ferry ; he was forced to attribute it to the French attacks on the Ferry ministry and to the ability of Malet, who was strongly supported by the Princess Imperial. [3]

The temporary estrangement was, however, soon followed by an even more passionate advance. On November 15 Malet came to consult Bismarck about Egypt and asked him if he would not urge the French to be reasonable. Bismarck refused to take sides : if the negotiations broke down, both France and England would put the blame on him : if he were sure of English support against France, he would risk it, but he had no faith in England " since Mr. Gladstone's uncalled for and unprovoked attack upon

[1] Courcel to Ferry, telegram, Nov. 12, 1884. D.D.F. vol. v. No. 450, pp. 469-70.

[2] Ferry to Courcel, telegram, Nov. 14, 1884. D.D.F. vol. v. No. 451, pp. 470-71.

[3] Courcel to Ferry, private, Nov. 26, 1884. D.D.F. vol. v. No. 467, p. 489.

Austria and Germany previously to his accession to office"
(this had not prevented his supporting English policy in
Egypt in 1882 and 1883). He advised the English government to come to a definite agreement with France—perhaps
France would make financial concessions in Egypt in
return for English mediation in China.[1] Granville proceeded to act on this advice and approached Waddington,
the French ambassador at London, on November 24; as an
attempt to mediate between France and China he produced some very unsatisfactory terms which he had received from the Chinese and then went on to say that he
would like to arrive at a preliminary agreement with
France about Egyptian finances, an agreement which Bismarck had said he would see with pleasure.[2] Ferry, with
the impression of Bismarck's annoyance still fresh in his
mind, was afraid that France was about to be left in the
lurch and he telegraphed to Courcel on November 25 for
an explanation.[3]

Bismarck, however, gave the explanation without being
asked ; one of his most remarkable gifts was his ability
to divine what was in the other man's mind and thus to
create a good effect by explaining things away before ever
an explanation was demanded. When, on November 27,
Courcel arrived, full of indignation, Bismarck did not give
him time to open his mouth, but said at once that he wanted
to speak to him about Egypt. About a week ago Malet had
come to him for advice, but he had refused to take sides :
parliamentary governments both in France and England
were too unstable to risk close co-operation with them ; as
Francis I. said of women, *bien fol est qui s'y fie.* He had

---

[1] Malet to Granville, most confidential, Nov. 15, 1884. F.O. 64/1052 ;
private, Nov. 15, 1884. G.D. 29/179.

[2] Waddington to Ferry, telegram, Nov. 24, 1884. D.D.F. vol. v.
No. 462, pp. 484-6.

[3] Ferry to Courcel, telegram, Nov. 25, 1884. D.D.F. vol. v. No. 463,
p. 486.

hinted to the English that something might be done to
mollify the French by offering an international financial
control in Egypt and English mediation in China ; but he
did not believe that the Egyptian question would ever be
solved except by a European conference and the French
ought to summon such a conference to Paris, it would
flatter the French *amour-propre*. After three-quarters of an
hour Courcel managed to get in a word : the use Granville
had made of Bismarck's advice had given the French the
impression that they were being left alone with England.
Bismarck put on a fine display of fury : the English, by
saying nothing of international control, had abused the
charitable alms he had given to their spiritual poverty ;
Gladstone and Granville were the coxcombs of politics—
" they are like old beaux who live on the reputation of
successes they have never had ". Courcel was now in a
better temper and recapitulated to Bismarck the French
attitude—France was not prepared to be bought off by
English mediation in China, but she could not oppose
England in Egypt alone and, unless supported by the other
powers, France would have to settle with England and
indeed make an alliance with her (" the entente established
on the banks of the Nile will necessarily tend to take on the
proportions of a general agreement on every question and
the character of a close alliance "—a curious prophecy of
future developments). This was Bismarck's opportunity :
France, he said, did not need to stand alone against England ; she could have German support whenever she
wanted it—" I want you to forgive Sedan, as after 1815 you
came to forgive Waterloo " ; but France had rejected the
proffered friendship—" Your government is afraid of being
compromised ; it dare not appear in public arm-in-arm
with Germany ". Courcel replied that it was certainly
necessary to reckon with French sentiment, but that
there was enough good sense in France to appreciate the
results of practical co-operation with Germany ; they must

therefore work quietly together without being flamboyant about it.[1]

This remarkable conversation was on both sides a brilliant diplomatic performance. There can be little doubt that Bismarck, when he advised the English to approach France, had meant to provoke some sort of crisis or decision after the doubts of October. If the French were, as he complained to Courcel, so hostile to Germany that they were prepared to give way to England in Egypt rather than accept German support, then Bismarck would be well out of it: he would secure English gratitude and be at any rate on the way to restoring that second best, Anglo-French friendship. If, however, the French were determined not to settle with England, then he could insist that co-operation with Germany logically followed, and this is what he did in the conversation of November 27. But Courcel refused to be caught in this logical trap : he knew that German friendship " would have to be paid for ", and he had no desire to see France rush into an irrevocable quarrel with England, which would enable Bismarck to put up his price. The moral satisfaction of a conference at Paris was not enough—" If it succeeds, Bismarck will say we owe its success to his support ; if it fails, he will wash his hands of it and come to an arrangement with those who caused the failure ". France must therefore insist that the Egyptian dispute was a dispute between England and Europe, not between England and France. Nor did Courcel waver from his earlier principle of co-operation on concrete issues only, and Bismarck's remarks about forgiving Sedan met with no response ; never forgive, never forget, Courcel wrote to Ferry,[2] must be their basic dogma, and only as a

[1] Courcel to Ferry, telegram, Nov. 27, 1884. D.D.F. vol. v. No. 468 ; telegram, Nov. 28, 1884, No. 469 ; telegram, Nov. 29, 1884, No. 471, pp. 489-97. Further details in Courcel to Ferry, private, Dec. 3, 1884, No. 475, pp. 501-3.

[2] Courcel to Ferry, private, Dec. 3, 1884. D.D.F. vol. v. No. 475, p. 503.

temporary expedient could they substitute the motto— *pacifier le présent, réserver l'avenir*. Lord Lyons, the British ambassador at Paris, exactly described the French attitude, when he wrote to Granville in January 1885 : " Bismarck and Ferry are *jouant au plus fin* with each other at our expense. Each seems to think that he can use the other to help in thwarting us, without risk to himself." [1] Lyons sometimes feared that Bismarck was working for a Franco-German entente as a prelude to a partition of Belgium and Holland ; [2] but he hit on the fundamental weakness of Bismarck's policy when he wrote to Granville : " The patronage of Bismarck overthrew the Freycinet Cabinet ; it is not strengthening Jules Ferry. . . . The *revanche* is still at the bottom of every French heart." [3]

[1] Lyons to Granville, private, Jan. 20, 1885. G.D. 29/174.
[2] Lyons to Granville, private, Nov. 4, 1884. G.D. 29/174.
[3] Lyons to Granville, private, Nov. 25, 1884. G.D. 29/174.

CHAPTER V

THE ANGLO-GERMAN CONFLICT OVER NEW GUINEA, DECEMBER 1884–MARCH 1885

By the end of November 1884 Bismarck had set out once more on his attempt to win over France to open co-operation with Germany, and the natural accompaniment, as in April and August, was renewed hostility to England. On November 29 he spoke angrily to Malet of Granville's wish to separate Germany and France—" any such wish would not only not be successful, but would draw Germany and France closer together ".[1] And a few days later Malet wrote : " His general tone towards us is neither cordial nor friendly ".[2] On December 5 Bismarck sent to Münster a dispatch, which closely resembled the famous dispatch of May 5 : the friendly phrases of Granville were all very well, but they did not correspond to the actions of the Colonial Office, and unless the Colonial Office changed its behaviour Germany would be unfriendly in the Egyptian question. The examples of English hostility were of the slightest— English agents were trying to cut off the German settlements in the Cameroons from the mountains, English agents were disturbing German relations with the natives in Samoa, and the appointment of Sir Charles Warren as Commissioner for Bechuanaland and " the neighbouring districts and lands " was the prelude to an attempt to confine South-West Africa to the coast.[3] The very vagueness of these grievances shows that Bismarck was still groping for the precise cause of conflict, and this he found

[1] Malet to Granville, private, Nov. 29, 1884. G.D. 29/179.
[2] Malet to Granville, private, Dec. 5, 1884. G.D. 29/179.
[3] Bismarck to Münster, Dec. 5, 1884. G.P. vol. iv. No. 756, pp. 91-3.

neither in West Africa nor in Samoa, but in New Guinea.

The island of New Guinea (now known as Papua) lies due north of Australia, being separated from Queensland by the Torres Strait. It is a land of great mountains and poor harbours, and is at the present day one of the few places where the adventurous may find inhabitants completely untouched by European influence. The western half of the island belonged to the Dutch East Indies ; the eastern half was ownerless and there seemed no reason why its condition should ever change unless its barrenness and remoteness should tempt some power to establish a penal settlement there. The Australian colonists were anxious to have no convicts in their neighbourhood and had made repeated, but unsuccessful, attempts to get the unappropriated area annexed by the British government.[1] The Colonial Office had always refused on the ground of expense, but had assured the colonial governments that New Guinea was perfectly safe from European interference.

To satisfy the Australians, Ampthill had mentioned New Guinea to Hatzfeldt in April 1883, and Hatzfeldt had " observed laughingly that Prince Bismarck, as I knew, had always and strongly resisted the national desire in Germany for the acquisition of Colonies, and that when in the future the present Government was no more, and the Party in favour of Colonies succeeded to Power in Germany, it appeared to him that England and France would have taken good care to leave them none to annex " ;[2] and as late as June 1884 Herbert Bismarck had referred to New Guinea as virtually English.[3] The Angra Pequena affair made it difficult to resist the Australian demand for annexation any longer, and on August 6 the British Cabinet

---

[1] Particularly in June and July 1883, on the unfounded rumour that Italy intended to establish a penal settlement.

[2] Ampthill to Granville, secret, No. 142, April 27, 1883. F.O. 64/1144.

[3] See p. 42.

decided to make New Guinea a British protectorate.[1]

Granville, however, was very anxious not to give new offence to Germany and on August 8 enquired of Münster whether Germany had any ambitions there; Münster knew very little about the question, but he was determined not to get into trouble again and said that he believed that there were some German traders established on the north coast.[2] Granville thereupon insisted that action should be postponed until the German government could express its opinion. Gladstone at first disliked deferring to Germany in this way;[3] but, after reading Herbert Bismarck's letter of August 30, he recognised that it would be wiser to consult the Germans.[4] Derby thought consulting Germany dangerous—" If Bismarck objects and we don't give way we are in an awkward position with him; if he objects and we do give way, the rage of the Australians will exceed all bounds. If he does not object, have we gained much ? "[5] And Childers, the Chancellor of the Exchequer, was also vocal on behalf of the colonists : " We are dealing, not with a poor mongrel population as in South Africa, but with men as English and as proud as ourselves ".[6] The question was not discussed by the Cabinet, as the members were all on holiday, but Granville got his way and the Colonial Office was not allowed to proceed with the annexation until Germany had been consulted. On September 17 the British chargé d'affaires in Berlin was told to inform the German government of the British intention,[7] and a few days later Granville wrote privately to Plessen, the German chargé

[1] Derby to Queen Victoria, Aug. 6, 1884. *Letters of Queen Victoria* (cited Q.V.L.), Second Series, vol. iii. p. 524.

[2] Granville to Ampthill, confidential, No. 225c, Aug. 9, 1884. F.O. 64/1144.

[3] Gladstone to Granville, Sept. 2, 1884. G.D. 29/128.

[4] Gladstone to Granville, Sept. 5, 1884. G.D. 29/128.

[5] Derby to Granville, Sept. 18, 1884. G.D. 29/120.

[6] Childers to Granville, Sept. 29, 1884. G.D. 29/119.

[7] Granville to Scott, No. 261, Sept. 17, 1884. F.O. 64/1144.

d'affaires, suggesting that the question of New Guinea be the subject of unofficial conversations between Herbert Bismarck (then in England) and a British representative, and added : " I can say that the instructions given to our representative would be drafted in a large and liberal spirit ".[1] This offer was not taken up ; instead Plessen, on September 27, protested against the British action as a whole. Granville, pushed on by the Colonial Office on one side and anxious to please the Germans on the other, devised a compromise, which was communicated to Berlin on October 7 : [2] the British protectorate was to be limited to the south coast of New Guinea "without prejudice to any territorial question beyond these limits " and a joint commission should be set up to determine the fate of the rest. No comment was made by the German government, and early in December Meade of the Colonial Office, who was in Berlin for the West African conference, suggested unofficially to Busch, the German under-secretary, that England would be willing to surrender the islands off the coast of South-West Africa if Germany would raise no objection to the extension of the British protectorate over the rest of New Guinea.[3] On December 20 the German government answered, but in an unexpected way : it became known that large tracts of the north and north-east coast of New Guinea had been placed under German protection— and that by the method of hoisting the flag, to which Bismarck had so much objected when it had been employed by others. Bismarck answered Meade's expostulations with a series of excuses so rambling and miscellaneous as to make it obvious that his principal concern was the quarrel itself. The British proposal of October, with its implied standstill, was, he said, new to him ; England had immense possessions in that part of the world and the English navy was

[1] Granville to Plessen, private, Sept. 25, 1884. F.O. 64/1144.
[2] Granville to Scott, No. 291, Oct. 7, 1884. F.O. 64/1145.
[3] Memorandum by Meade, Feb. 10, 1885. F.O. 64/1148.

strong enough to protect those possessions, and it was un-
worthy of England to grudge Germany a settlement on the
coast of New Guinea. He doubted the " supposed strong
feelings " of the colonists, and besides, " this strip of New
Guinea was very small and of little value to England. In any
case he had been treated badly by England whose actions
do not accord with her professions." [1] The argument that
he understood the words " without prejudice to any
territorial question beyond these limits " as applying only
to the English occurred to Bismarck later, and was first
used by Münster in a conversation with Granville on
January 3 ; [2] it is in any case difficult to reconcile this
argument with Bismarck's statement to Meade that the
October dispatch was new to him.

The Australian colonists, who had so often urged the
annexation of New Guinea only to be assured that there
was no danger of any other power forestalling England,
were of course furious, and the Colonial Office, who had
given these assurances on Granville's advice, were furious
also. The Colonial Office proposed that England should now
annex every scrap of New Guinea, where the German flag
had not been actually hoisted, and that the offer of a joint
commission to weigh rival claims should be withdrawn.
The German activity in New Guinea made the Colonial
Office fear renewed German activity in Africa, and they
were particularly apprehensive of German designs on St.
Lucia Bay, which might give the Germans contact with
the Transvaal ; the Gladstone government had given the
Transvaal independence, but even they drew the line at
direct contact with other European powers. The two questions—New Guinea and St. Lucia Bay—were discussed at
a Cabinet on January 3. The general effect of the German
action had been to make the members of the Cabinet much
more hostile to Germany than they had been the previous

[1] Memorandum by Meade, Dec. 24, 1884. F.O. 64/1145.
[2] Granville to Malet, No. 4A, Jan. 3, 1885. F.O. 64/1146.

June ; as Chamberlain put it : " I don't care about New Guinea, and I am not afraid of German colonisation, but I don't like to be cheeked by Bismarck or anyone else ".[1] Gladstone's position was not so precise. He was ready to agree that there had been some "careless impropriety" in the form of Bismarck's proceeding—" there appears to be an element in him which I do not wish to characterise ". But Gladstone objected to occupying territory in competition with Germany—"considering what we have got, I am against entering into a scramble for the remainder " ; and again : " there is a wild and irrational spirit abroad, to which for one I do not feel at all disposed to give in " ; and he wrote to the Queen : " Mr. Gladstone believes that herein [refusal to annex more territory] he is only a humble representative of convictions, which were not general only but universal among the Statesmen of the first thirty years of his political life ". Moreover, in regard to New Guinea, the existence of a German settlement would, he thought, make the Australians more amenable : " I see my way clearly to this, that German colonization will strengthen and not weaken our hold upon our Colonies and will make it very difficult for them to maintain the domineering tone to which their public organs are too much inclined ".[2]

Gladstone was not present at the Cabinet of January 3, but he approved of the very Gladstonian compromise at which the Cabinet arrived : the annexations both in New Guinea and South Africa were to be proceeded with, but any intention of competing with Germany was disclaimed and the Germans were to be told that the annexations had

[1] Chamberlain to Dilke, Dec. 29, 1884. Garvin, *Chamberlain*, vol. i. p. 497.

[2] Gladstone to Granville, Dec. 25 ; Dec. 26 ; Dec. 28, 1884. G.D. 29/128 ; Jan. 29, 1885. G.D. 29/129 ; Gladstone to Queen Victoria, Jan. 5, 1885. Q.V.L. vol. iii. p. 591 ; Jan. 23, 1885. Q.V.L. vol. iii. p. 593. Further evidence of Gladstone's attitude no doubt exists in the Gladstone papers ; but I was refused access to them on the ground that they are not available to the general public until 1940.

been undertaken practically as a favour to Germany. Granville reported to the Queen : " It was decided to advise Your Majesty to annex to Cape Colony the whole Coast line properly belonging to it but not to extend the annexations merely for the purpose of excluding the chance of the Germans settling there ".[1] As the whole coast-line properly belonging to Cape Colony was interpreted as extending to the Portuguese boundary near Delagoa Bay, the negative proviso seems a little empty. In regard to New Guinea, the sharply worded draft for Berlin, which had been prepared by Pauncefote and the Colonial Office, was considerably amended ; to the announcement of the new British annexations was added the sentence : " The recent action of Her Majesty's Government has been prompted in a great measure by the desire to obviate all the inconveniences that might arise from an absence of jurisdiction on the Coast of New Guinea between the limits of the British and German Protectorates ". The offer to proceed with the proposed Commission was shorn of its offensive phrase (" notwithstanding that the occupation by Germany of the most important islands and groups has relieved it of its main labours ") and a conciliatory phrase substituted (" with a view to clearing up the question, and removing chances of differences between the two Governments "). This important dispatch should have been sent off at once, but there was some confusion whether the Cabinet amendments were to be drafted by the Colonial or the Foreign Office ; Derby could not be consulted, as he had retired to Knowsley without a secretary, and " he dislikes telegraphs " ; so the dispatch did not go until January 13.[2]

The estrangement between England and Germany had naturally been followed by Courcel with extreme interest. The coolness of October, and certain differences of opinion

[1] Granville to Queen Victoria, Jan. 3, 1885. G.D. 29/45.
[2] Granville to Malet, No. 23, Jan. 13, 1885. F.O. 64/1146. Pauncefote's draft is Dec. 30, 1884. F.O. 64/1145.

between France and Germany at the West African conference, had made Courcel circumspect, and as late as
December 27 he wrote to Ferry that any friendship with
Germany would be a stormy one unless it was accompanied
by complete submission to German wishes.[1] Nor did the
colonial conflict make him less suspicious : colonial concessions by England, he wrote on January 11, might easily
make Bismarck more amenable in regard to Egypt.[2] But
the leading part taken by Bismarck in demanding in-
demnities for the bombardment of Alexandria, and Bismarck's open pleasure at the difficulties which the Russian
advance in Asia was creating for the English, made Courcel
less suspicious : Bismarck was aiming, he thought, at
nothing less than the destruction of the British Empire, and
" late events have practically convinced me that he has
carried things too far with England to turn back easily and
let us down ". But Bismarck would always aim at keeping
France obedient by threatening to settle with England, and
the danger of such a reconciliation might very well arise
with a change of ministry in England, especially if there
followed a Radical ministry with Herbert Bismarck's
friend, Chamberlain, at its head.[3] Courcel therefore refused
to move from his position of reserve : as he told Bismarck
on January 19, co-operation between France and Germany
must continue to be *von Fall zu Fall*. Bismarck seems to
have thought (wrongly) that Ferry would be less suspicious,
for he suggested meeting him in Switzerland or in the south
of France ; [4] but the idea was not pursued and Bismarck's
more serious method of convincing the French was to make

[1] Courcel to Ferry, private, Dec. 27, 1884. D.D.F. vol. v. No. 500,
p. 525.

[2] Courcel to Ferry, private, Jan. 11, 1885. D.D.F. vol. v. No. 518,
pp. 541-2.

[3] Courcel to Ferry, private, Jan. 19, 1885. D.D.F. vol. v. No. 528,
pp. 550-54.

[4] Courcel to Ferry, confidential, Jan. 20, 1885. D.D.F. vol. v. No.
530, pp. 555-8.

his conflict with England even more violent.

The opportunity was provided by Malet's communication on January 24 of the British Note concerning New Guinea. " Wherever Germany has endeavoured to found a colony ", Bismarck exclaimed, " England has closed in " ; in the dispatch of May 5 (parts of which he read) he had, he said, offered England the support of Germany in return for assistance in German colonial enterprises, and, when he found that Münster had completely failed to convey to Granville the importance which his government attached to the Colonial question, he had sent his son Herbert to London, but without any result other than personal expressions of good-will. Malet enquired what exactly Germany wanted—New Guinea ? Zululand ? The answer was of course neither the one nor the other, but a grievance. Bismarck said " that the understanding which he had arrived at with France in consequence of his failure to come to one with us, put it out of his power to take up the question now, as he had expounded it to us in May, and that he could no longer make any particular bargain ".[1] Malet shrewdly suspected that the alleged understanding with France did not exist ; [2] but he naturally accepted without question Bismarck's criticism of Münster. It would be pertinent to ask why, if Münster was so largely responsible for the misunderstanding between the two countries, Bismarck did not recall him either now or earlier ; but the question requires no answer.

The German attitude was further defined in dispatches which Bismarck addressed the same day to Münster and Hohenlohe. German opposition to England in Egypt, he wrote to Münster, was entirely due to the unfriendly

[1] Malet to Granville, No. 45, Jan. 24, 1885. F.O. 64/1146. Bismarck's reference to the dispatch of May 5 is the origin of the " bogey document " story. Bismarck can have read only a very short extract from the dispatch or Malet would have reported the reference to Heligoland.

[2] Malet to Granville, private, Jan. 24, 1885, G.D. 29/179.

colonial policy of England, and, if Granville put off Münster
with polite phrases while England committed further unfriendly acts—" taking away part of the north of New
Guinea which has already been conceded to us and re-
viving obsolete rights in the Portuguese fashion at St.
Lucia Bay, where England never had any business "—
relations would grow even worse.[1] To Hohenlohe, Bismarck
wrote that the object of German policy concerning Egypt
was to convince Ferry that France could rely on Germany.[2]
Hohenlohe reported optimistically, after a conversation
with Ferry, that Ferry was completely satisfied : " His
confidence in Your Highness's intentions is unshaken, and
he is far removed from the mistrust usual here, which
makes the average Frenchman suspect perfidious plans
and traps of German policy everywhere ".[3] The alarm with
which Ferry received at this moment a proposal for German
mediation in China, conveyed unofficially by Bleichroeder,
suggests that Hohenlohe was mistaken.[4]

Münster in London performed his task to the best of his
ability. He passed on to Granville the substance of the
dispatches of January 24 and 25, a little toned down it is
true,[5] and he presented a strong note objecting to the
English annexations in New Guinea.[6] This note drew from
Gladstone the tribute : " Bismarck shows in it that he is a
perfect master of the art of involving a question in a cloud

[1] Bismarck to Münster, Jan. 24, 1885. G.P. vol. iv. No. 757 ; Jan.
25, 1885. G.P. vol. iv. No. 758, pp. 93-9.

[2] Bismarck to Hohenlohe, Jan. 24, 1885. G.P. vol. iii. No. 697, p. 441.

[3] Hohenlohe to Bismarck, Jan. 27, 1885. G.P. vol. iii. No. 698,
pp. 441-3.

[4] Note by Ferry on Courcel to Ferry, private, Jan. 22, 1885. D.D.F.
vol. v. No. 535, pp. 566-7.

[5] Granville to Malet, No. 61A, Jan. 29, 1885. F.O. 64/1073, where
Münster is reported to have said : " The conduct of the English Govern-
ment in Colonial matters had made Germany less desirous of assisting
England in the Egyptian question ".

[6] Münster to Granville, Jan. 28, 1885. F.O. 64/1147.

of words, as well as of plain and laconic speech, according as he may desire the one or the other ".[1] Granville's replies were as benevolent as ever, though no more likely to satisfy Bismarck. In regard to New Guinea, he urged that there had been a mutual misunderstanding,[2] and he sent to Malet a long dispatch defending his conduct and assuring Bismarck that England would welcome German colonial expansion; even some members of the Cabinet thought this rather far-fetched, and it certainly had no effect on Bismarck.[3]

Throughout February Anglo-German relations remained in this unsatisfactory state, and Franco-German co-operation over Egypt continued with increasing success. Malet and Bismarck had a number of sharp interviews, but without any useful result, and when Malet tried to start a practical discussion about New Guinea, Bismarck "suddenly changed the conversation ".[4] Münster presented another Note on February 23, demanding the cancellation of the later English annexations in New Guinea,[5] and he had an argumentative interview with Granville on February 24,[6] in which he expressed Bismarck's latest grievance—that the

[1] Gladstone to Granville, Feb. 3, 1885. G.D. 29/129.

[2] Granville to Münster, Feb. 7, 1885. F.O. 64/1147.

[3] Granville to Malet, Feb. 7, 1885. F.O. 64/1147. To the sentence, " Her Majesty's Govt. have had no reason whatever to oppose German colonisation and a vast field was open to Germany both in the East and the West without entrenching on the legitimate sphere of action of Great Britain ", Kimberley appended the comment : " We can hardly be said not to have opposed in New Guinea and Zululand — and I cannot see that any ' vast ' field is now open to colonization. Also ' legitimate sphere of action ' involves difficult doctrines and is much open to question." The sentence was modified by changing " had no reason whatever " to " generally had no reason " and the word " vast " omitted.

[4] Malet to Granville, private, Feb. 7, 1885; private, Feb. 26, 1885. G.D. 29/179.

[5] Münster to Granville, Feb. 23, 1885. F.O. 64/1148.

[6] Granville to Malet, No. 130, Feb. 25, 1885. F.O. 64/1148.

British Notes were too long and too frequent; statesmen " overburdened with business " therefore overlooked important statements, and misunderstandings arose. Münster, rather late in the day, was now doing his best to insist on the gravity of the German grievances, and really expected to be recalled at any moment.[1] The New Guinea question was at a complete deadlock; but Pauncefote discussed the matter unofficially with Krauel, of the German Foreign Office, when he met him on other business, and the two had no difficulty in sketching a solution—that a line (ultimately the 8th degree of latitude was agreed on) should be fixed beyond which each side should withdraw.

Except for Münster's conversations with Granville— hardly a reliable indication—there is no evidence concerning Bismarck's policy throughout February. The *Grosse Politik* is silent, and Bismarck had no conversations with Courcel, which might have filled the gap. It almost seemed as though the diplomatic development was completed : Germany and France were working confidently together in the Egyptian question and the fruits of this co-operation would no doubt make France readier for further co-operation in the future. But it was not in Bismarck's nature to let a situation stand still ; the open estrangement between England and Germany having lasted a month, it was time to bring it to an end. This would be a useful hint to the French that Germany was not irrevocably committed to quarrelling with England; but on the other hand the settlement of a particular dispute would by no means preclude fresh disputes in the future. On February 27 Granville was provoked in the House of Lords into saying that Bismarck had often advised England to *take Egypt*. This gave Bismarck the opportunity of replying in the Reichstag on March 2 that he had always advised England to deal with Egypt in co-operation with Turkey, its suzerain ; [2] England,

---

[1] Dilke to Granville, Feb. 24, 1885. G.D. 29/122.

[2] This was untrue : Bismarck certainly suggested to Salisbury that

he declared, was trying in vain to sow distrust between Germany and France, and he passed on to give a highly coloured version of the Anglo-German colonial disputes. This public outburst was obviously designed to raise the market; for immediately afterwards (on March 4) Herbert Bismarck was sent over to England to settle the question of New Guinea. The visit was a repetition of the visit in June of the previous year: Herbert Bismarck began in a tone of exaggerated rudeness—he told Dilke, for example, that he had come over to " try to force us to dismiss Lord Granville and Lord Derby " [1]—and ended in a tone of exaggerated friendliness. He had four interviews with Granville, which began with a great deal of sterile recrimination, but which finally led to a satisfactory agreement.[2] Granville read over to Herbert Bismarck the speech he was about to make in the House of Lords correcting his remarks of February 27 ; Germany was to drop her opposition concerning St. Lucia Bay, and England would undertake not to oppose Germany in the Cameroons ; New Guinea was to be partitioned as Pauncefote and Krauel had suggested ; and, Bismarck's health having improved, he would see ambassadors more often and the exchange of lengthy Notes was to cease. At the conclusion Granville said that " the behaviour of the German government was strikingly friendly " ; Herbert Bismarck's judgement, as expressed a few days later, was that " nothing could exceed the kindness of Lord Granville and our [the British] Government, and he felt he had brought back excellent news and good seed for the future ".[3]

England should *take Egypt* and let Russia have the Straits ; it has, however, been argued that Bismarck in this speech was referring only to advice given to the Gladstone government.

[1] Gwynn and Tuckwell, *Dilke*, vol. ii. p. 99.

[2] Partially reported in Herbert Bismarck to Bismarck, March 7, 1885. G.P. vol. iv. No. 760, pp. 100-102 ; and more completely in Granville to Scott, No. 96A, March 9, 1885. F.O. 64/1149.

[3] Scott to Sanderson, private, March 14, 1885. G.D. 29/179.

Herbert Bismarck had conversations with a number of other Cabinet ministers, all in a rather rambling and desultory manner. Gladstone went out of his way to express to Herbert Bismarck his sympathy with German colonial expansion ; but Gladstone's " lack of understanding of foreign policy " was a Bismarckian dogma, and Herbert Bismarck hardly troubled to mention Gladstone's remarks in his report. It might have been worth his while to record Gladstone's statement that England would find it more difficult to be friendly to German claims if they were presented as blackmail.[1] It is curious also to find Herbert Bismarck denying to Hartington that Bismarck had any personal hostility to Gladstone : " I showed him convincingly that there could be no question of this and reminded him of the similar yarn which had been circulated concerning Prince Gortchakov". Herbert Bismarck also had a conversation with Waddington, in which his desire to emphasise the importance (and the dictatorial character) of his visit led him to make some very unwise remarks ; for he told Waddington that he had been using the Egyptian question to wring colonial concessions from England, and Waddington did not much like France being used as an instrument for German blackmail.   The reconciliation between England and Germany was announced to the world on March 12, when, during the debate on the Foreign Office vote, Gladstone gave his blessing to German colonial enterprise and announced his readiness to redress any future grievances as soon as they arose.

[1] Gladstone to Granville, March 5, 1885. G.D. 29/128.

CHAPTER VI

THE ABORTIVE DISPUTE OVER ZANZIBAR AND THE END OF THE FRANCO-GERMAN ENTENTE, APRIL–OCTOBER 1885

THAT the German opposition to England in the Egyptian question had been solely due to colonial difficulties had been a commonplace in Bismarck's communications to London since the beginning of the year, and Herbert Bismarck had assured Gladstone that German opposition would cease as soon as the New Guinea dispute was satisfactorily settled.[1] But on the news of the agreement between England and Germany, Courcel reassured Ferry: German friendship, he wrote, would always be uncertain and Bismarck no doubt wished to warn the French that he could do without them; but the idea of a general settlement was "scarcely admissible", and what had happened was only a truce, not even a stage on the way to good relations. New colonial difficulties would soon arise—Courcel mentioned in particular Zanzibar—and Germany, to complete her continental policy and her industrial development, would inevitably be led to absorb Holland and the Dutch Empire, bribing France with Belgium. These projects were not yet ripe; but in the meantime Germany would continue to embarrass England by supporting France over Egypt and encouraging Russia in Central Asia.[2]

Courcel's expectations proved correct : the settlement of the New Guinea affair did not make German opposition

[1] Gladstone to Granville, March 6, 1885. G.D. 29/128.

[2] Courcel to Ferry, private, March 11, 1885. D.D.F. vol. v. No. 622, pp. 646-50. Lyons's apprehensions about Holland and Belgium were also renewed at this time : Lyons to Granville, private, March 13, 1885. G.D. 29/174.

in regard to Egypt diminish. Granville wrote to Lyons on March 14 : " Bismarck is behaving as ill as possible. After this Mission of Peace and a complete making up, creating difficulties at the last moment about Egyptian Finance, concerning which he had promised that no objection would be raised by Germany, if France and England agreed." [1] Bismarck's part in the Anglo-Russian conflict over Afghanistan, which came to a head in the spring of 1885, is more difficult to assess. Eyre Crowe asserts that the troubles with Russia in Central Asia were " directly fomented by a German special mission to St. Petersburgh " ; [2] of this there is no evidence, but Crowe's statements, though sometimes exaggerated, usually contain a basis of truth. No argument can be based upon the absence of evidence in the *Grosse Politik*, nor upon the letter in which, after war had been averted, Bismarck assured the Emperor that Germany had done nothing " to increase the chances of war ".[3] Bismarck certainly knew of the Russian plans, for he spoke of them with approval to Courcel ; [4] and it is obvious that if Russia and England had to quarrel it was far better for Bismarck that they should do so in Central Asia than in the Near East, where Austria would have been drawn in. It is further true that in the war crisis of April 1885 Bismarck performed a great service to Russia by urging Turkey not to open the Straits to England, and by getting Austria and France to give the same advice. But it is not necessary to ascribe this to an anti-English motive : Bismarck had no choice if he was to preserve the League of the Three Emperors and to prevent France outbidding him for Russian friendship.

The Anglo-Russian crisis temporarily reduced Bismarck's interest in his relations with the Western Powers ; and

[1] Granville to Lyons, private, March 14, 1885. G.D. 29/204.
[2] Memorandum by Crowe, Jan. 1, 1907. B.D. vol. iii. p. 408.
[3] Bismarck to William I., May 27, 1885. G.P. vol. iv. No. 777, p. 125.
[4] D.D.F. vol. v. pp. 557 and 649.

when it terminated, early in May, the situation had been
altered by the fall of Ferry. In the last days of March
Ferry's Chinese policy ended in disaster : the French forces
were defeated at Lang-Son, and the news of the defeat,
greatly exaggerated by those French parties who had
opposed Ferry's colonial policy, led to the overthrow of
Ferry in the Chamber on March 30. Ferry's colonial policy
had been criticised because it seemed to be making France
dependent on Germany ; but it was not known at the time
that Ferry had asked Germany to exert her influence on
China,[1] nor that Hatzfeldt had dropped a very discreet hint
to the Chinese minister.[2] It was the suspicion, not the
knowledge, of German patronage which discredited Ferry ;
and this would not have been enough to cause his fall if
the colonial policy, based on German acquiescence, had not
seemingly ended in failure. It is fair to add that in fact
peace was concluded immediately after Ferry's fall, not
because of German influence, but because the Chinese
government was sincerely anxious to finish the war. Later,
and particularly after the revelation in December 1885 of
Ferry's appeal to Germany, the fall of the Ferry government came to be regarded as a manifestation of French
distrust of Germany ; at the time it appeared simply the
result of a lost battle—much as the death of Gordon shook
the Gladstone ministry in England.

Certainly Bismarck did not at once draw the moral that
his policy of Franco-German co-operation had failed. He
had, it is true, come to count on Ferry, had indeed exaggerated the degree to which Ferry reciprocated his own
friendly feelings ;[3] but he lost no time in assuring Courcel

[1] Ferry to Courcel, telegram, March 29, 1885. D.D.F. vol. v. No.
638, p. 660.

[2] Memorandum by Hatzfeldt, March 31, 1885. G.P. vol. iii. No.
700, pp. 444-5.

[3] Scott to Granville, private, April 4, 1885. G.D. 29/179 : " Bismarck
is, I hear, much taken aback by the change of Government in France, as

that German policy would not change, and Courcel telegraphed to Freycinet, Ferry's successor, on April 11 : " He
asked me to express to you the confidence that the relations
lately established between France and Germany would
undergo no alteration ".[1] Early in May Bismarck renewed
to Freycinet the proposals for a continental league against
England which he had often made to Ferry. In a conversation with Courcel, on May 10, Bismarck was as outspoken
as he had been on previous occasions. He began by complaining that Freycinet was deferring too much to England :
he, Bismarck, went to the trouble of persuading Russia and
Austria to support a French proposal and then found that
Freycinet had already given way—" I cannot be more
French than the French ". Germany could easily be on
good terms with England—" our interests are nowhere
divergent except perhaps in colonial questions in which she
has been stupid enough to oppose us, but which could easily
be settled finally in a friendly way "; but Germany was at
the moment trying to balance English maritime supremacy
by a union of the continental powers, especially in the
Egyptian question. There the support of France was
necessary; if, however, France tried to settle with England,
Germany would compete with her for English friendship,
and Germany would win—" France could only offer England what she already had in abundance, colonial and
maritime strength, whereas Germany was in a position to
give her the continental support she needed ". Bismarck
was thus seeking the friendship of France by means of
threats : France must co-operate with Germany against
England, otherwise Germany would co-operate with England against France. It was a curious, though very German,
way of offering an alliance ; but an offer it certainly was,

he relied chiefly on M. Ferry for the maintenance of the ' entente
cordiale ' and had a very high idea of his prudence ".

[1] Courcel to Freycinet, telegram, April 11, 1885. D.D.F. vol. vi.
No. 6, p. 6.

and, as on the occasion of earlier offers, Courcel went to Paris in order to discuss the reply with Freycinet in person.[1]

Ferry has been sometimes presented as the only exponent, or at any rate practitioner, of the entente with Germany ; but there was little to choose between Ferry's policy and that of Freycinet. Like Ferry, Freycinet was quite ready to alarm England with stories of a European coalition against her—Lyons's letters to Granville in May are full of references to this danger ; [2] but neither Ferry nor Freycinet meant to go the whole way towards an entente with Germany and neither was averse from settling with England if the terms were good enough. The instructions from Freycinet with which Courcel returned to Berlin were very similar to those which he had received from Ferry on similar occasions : co-operation with Germany on concrete issues, but no flaunting of the entente and no opposition to England merely for the sake of opposing her.[3] Such a policy of co-operation within limits had not altogether satisfied Bismarck when it had been pursued by Ferry; but after an interval of reserve (particularly in October 1884) Bismarck had accepted what Ferry was prepared to offer, and Freycinet might reasonably anticipate the same reception.

Courcel's return to Berlin coincided with the arrival of an English emissary, specially dispatched to ascertain Bismarck's grievance. The British government had accepted without demur Herbert Bismarck's statement that New Guinea was now the only question separating the two

[1] Courcel to Freycinet, confidential, May 10, 1885. D.D.F. vol. vi. No. 23, pp. 21-7.

[2] Lyons to Granville, private, May 15, May 19, May 29, 1885. G.D. 29/174. All refer to the European coalition which Bismarck was trying to form against England.

[3] There are no actual instructions to Courcel in D.D.F. vol. vi., but Freycinet's policy was explained by Courcel to Bismarck on May 22. Courcel to Freycinet, confidential, May 24, 1885. D.D.F. vol. vi. No. 37, p. 33.

countries; the question of New Guinea had been settled, but Bismarck's policy remained as unfriendly as before ; obviously, therefore, there must be some other colonial question in which England had offended, and this too must be removed in order to recover Bismarck's friendship. Barely two months had elapsed since Herbert Bismarck's special visit to England; it was too soon to expect another. But Granville held firmly (or as firmly as he could) to the view that Bismarck was anxious to be friendly to England, if only the English would let him : there could be no question, therefore, of negotiation through the ordinary diplomatic channels. The next best thing to a visit from Herbert Bismarck was to send Rosebery, Herbert's close friend and a recent addition to the Cabinet, to Berlin; and to Berlin Rosebery went in the last days of May.[1] As had been anticipated, Bismarck had once more a colonial grievance : this time it was East Africa.

The entire coast of East Africa down to the frontier of Portuguese East Africa was regarded by the British as belonging to the Sultan of Zanzibar, a Mohammedan prince, whose power was declining even more rapidly than that of the other Mohammedan rulers in Africa. The British were solely concerned to prevent a threat to the route to India or such expansion on the mainland as would open a back door to the Nile. England and France had a long-standing agreement to leave Zanzibar alone, but to this agreement Germany was not a party ; and, as in other cases, the British government had considered forestalling the Germans.[2] They had refrained, partly to avoid difficulties with

[1] It is not possible to be very precise as to the details of Rosebery's visits. Bismarck made no record of the conversations—or it has not been published ; Rosebery promised Granville a full report, but the Gladstone government fell before it was written. Still, the references in Granville's correspondence give a reliable general impression.

[2] *E.g.* Kimberley to Granville, Nov. 24, 1884. G.D. 29/136 : " I see rumours that the Germans have designs on Zanzibar. In ordinary circs. one would pay no attention to them, but the Germans show such

the French, but mainly because of repeated German assurances that they had no designs on Zanzibar; as late as March 6, 1885, Herbert Bismarck had said to Dilke: " I was empowered to say that nothing lay further from us than to interfere with the independence of Zanzibar ".[1] Now, however, it appeared that by Zanzibar the Germans had meant the island and that alone; the entire mainland they regarded as ownerless, though they rather weakened their case by referring to the question as the Zanzibar question until its final settlement in 1890. The British consular officials in Zanzibar naturally disliked this German activity, and they had undoubtedly encouraged the Sultan to reassert his somewhat musty rights on the mainland. It was to this that Bismarck objected. He admitted to Rosebery that he had been thwarting England in every way, but declared that he was quite willing to be friendly if England helped him in Zanzibar.[2] Rosebery, however, had the impression that Bismarck had become more friendly because he had been " influenced by an unsatisfactory conversation with Courcel ".[3] This seems a more plausible explanation, particularly as nothing was done about Zanzibar: the Gladstone government was out of office before it had time to make this new surrender to Germany, and the Zanzibar question continued to cause sporadic ill-feeling between England and Germany.

But Courcel's reports give a very different picture: there Bismarck's change of policy is ascribed in large part to the

an aggressive spirit that we cannot tell what they may do next. Besides Zanzibar might have a particular attraction to Bismarck as being a quarter where German interference would be specially disagreeable to England.

" We ought I think to do our utmost to prevent any foreign power supplanting us at Zanzibar."

[1] G.P. vol. iv. p. 104.

[2] Rosebery to Granville, May 30, 1885. G.D. 29/117.

[3] Granville to Gladstone, May 29, 1885. G.D. 29/129 ; to Lyons, May 30, 1885. G.D. 29/204.

influence of Rosebery. Courcel's first interview with Bismarck on his return from Paris was on May 22. Courcel developed Freycinet's policy of co-operation with Germany on concrete issues. Bismarck says that he received from Courcel the impression that the new French government was not likely to oppose England with resolution; according to Courcel, Bismarck expressed his confidence in Freycinet personally, but doubted his remaining long in office. But Bismarck did not seem annoyed or estranged: he was quite ready, he said, to work with Freycinet when the French government had consolidated its position; almost his last words were : " Let us keep quiet until the autumn. Then we shall see." [1] Hatzfeldt told Courcel on May 26 that Bismarck was a little disappointed at the French reluctance to follow a policy of relentless opposition to England—" The Chancellor finds that you don't want to play *le grand jeu* "— but Courcel did not detect any coldness on the German side and, as late as May 27, was confident that Rosebery's visit had been a complete failure.[2]

On May 28 there was a dramatic *dénouement*. Bismarck sent for Courcel and said he wanted to speak to him on a very intimate and confidential matter: the Emperor was very ill, his bladder trouble was acute, he would probably die. And then—we are in for an era of Coburgs. The new Emperor, who was completely ignorant of realities, would scrap Bismarck's policy, and Bismarck would be too old to educate him in the right way; he had done it with the old Emperor, but now—" I am not strong enough any more, I have not the health ". The new reign would see an entente between Germany and England, and Bismarck wanted to warn the French now, so that they could make up their

[1] Courcel to Freycinet, confidential, May 24, 1885. D.D.F. vol. vi. No. 27, pp. 32-7 ; Bismarck to Hohenlohe, May 25, 1885. G.P. vol. iii. No. 702, pp. 445-6.

[2] Courcel to Freycinet, confidential, May 27, 1885. D.D.F. vol. vi. No. 28, pp. 37-40.

quarrel with England and not feel tricked and deserted when the change of German policy came; "if our old Emperor is spared there will be no change . . . but I want to warn you". In any case, Bismarck continued, he thought Freycinet would not mind following his advice : " Ever since he has been minister I have had a feeling that your government has been softer towards England ". He had, he said, already told Rosebery that France and England should settle Egypt between them. Apart from that he had not discussed politics with Rosebery, and he did not think that Rosebery had been entrusted with any mission by his government; it was merely a private visit, perhaps designed to add to Rosebery's prestige in England ; the change of policy had nothing to do with Rosebery, the stone in the Emperor's bladder was the sole cause. And then reverting to the Emperor's health, he exclaimed : " If I lost him, the world would never be the same for me again ! " His chin trembled convulsively, the blood rushed to his cheeks, and his eyes filled with tears. Later in the afternoon there was rather an anticlimax, for Hatzfeldt, to whom Courcel gave an account of the conversation, was very surprised and unguardedly remarked that he did not think the Emperor was so ill, nor Bismarck so estranged from the Crown Prince.[1]

Of this remarkable conversation one thing may be said with certainty, that Bismarck was warning the French that he was about to change his policy and become more friendly to England. The cause of this change is hardly to be found in the Emperor's bladder trouble, about which no more was heard. Courcel thought Rosebery's visit had something to do with it. But Rosebery, far from taking the credit, thought the change due to Courcel. Besides, what could Rosebery have said of the slightest importance ? That England would not oppose German colonial expansion ? There was nothing

[1] Courcel to Freycinet, strictly personal and confidential for the minister, May 28, 1885. D.D.F. vol. vi. No. 29, pp. 40-47.

very novel about that ; moreover, the colonial difficulties
were part of Bismarck's policy, not the cause of it, and
Bismarck, not the English, dropped Zanzibar after Rosebery's visit. Rosebery may have hinted at the possibility of
his becoming Foreign Secretary on the retirement of Gladstone (which was regarded as imminent), and the prospect
of Rosebery, the admiring and admired friend of Herbert
Bismarck, as Foreign Secretary might influence Bismarck
towards a more pro-English attitude. It is less likely that
Rosebery foretold the fall of Gladstone and the succession
of Salisbury, which took place a fortnight later : it was
hardly a thing Rosebery would boast of, even had he expected it; it was almost entirely unexpected; and in any
case no one at this time expected a Tory government to
last more than a few months, the Liberal split over Home
Rule being yet in the future.

These speculations are not very remunerative : Bismarck's policy towards England for the last twelve months
had not been determined by English colonial policy or the
offences of individual ministers, but by the desire to stand
well with France, and therefore there was nothing of importance that Rosebery could say. The only reason for
supposing that Rosebery's visit had something to do with
Bismarck's change of policy is that Bismarck went out of
his way to emphasise to Courcel that it had nothing to do
with his change of policy. But, in his own characteristic way,
Bismarck may have been misleading Courcel by simply
telling the truth : certainly Courcel drew the conclusion
that Rosebery's visit had been important, which was perhaps what Bismarck wanted him to think. Then had
French policy changed ? Bismarck affected to believe it
had—" you have become softer to England "; but, as Freycinet replied to Courcel : " Our only action has been to
break with the system of gratuitous annoyances and useless provocations of England . . . which compromised the
good relations of France with her natural ally without

compensation ".[1] Certainly Freycinet had hesitated to swallow the German bait whole ; but Ferry had hesitated as much, and Bismarck had found Ferry's hesitation perfectly natural. Ferry, like Freycinet, had continued to negotiate with England and had used his good relations with Germany to get better terms out of England. Nothing in French policy in May suggested a change of policy. It is, however, true that Courcel had been more anxious to co-operate with Germany than either Ferry or Freycinet; and he may well have expressed to Bismarck more disappoint-ment at Ferry's fall and Freycinet's reserve than appears in his reports. Freycinet certainly suspected this, and his dispatch of June 15, in which he asserted his continuity of policy, was largely a rebuke to Courcel.

But Courcel's pessimism about French policy would not have made Bismarck give up unless he had wanted to give up. Bismarck's change of policy was not due to any particular event, but to the growing conviction that his policy was not going to work. Courcel probably came near the mark when he attributed Bismarck's change to the unwillingness of both France and Russia to push their quarrels with England to extremes ; the prospect of a European coalition against England had failed to tempt them. Bismarck had hoped that France would draw steadily nearer to Germany; instead France had reached a certain point and then stopped. Freycinet's offence, in fact, was not that he abandoned Ferry's policy, but that he con-tinued it : Bismarck was getting " no forrarder ". It was, therefore, only to be expected that Bismarck would draw back and establish more cordial relations with England. But there is no reason to suppose that the reconciliation with England was meant to be any more final than the " final " settlement of Angra Pequena in June 1884 or of New Guinea in March 1885. Nothing would have been

[1] Freycinet to Courcel, June 15, 1885. D.D.F. vol. vi. No. 36, pp. 55-6.

easier than to tell Courcel that the Emperor was completely
recovered and a change of policy therefore unnecessary;
and had circumstances remained unchanged Bismarck
might well have acted on his remark to Courcel—" let us
wait until the autumn and then we shall see ". But during
the following months the European situation changed pro-
foundly. In the middle of June the Gladstone government
fell, and Salisbury at once expressed his anxiety to co-
operate with Germany.[1] This was not in itself of great
importance, for Bismarck had in the past expressed himself as critically of Salisbury as of Gladstone, and his letter
of July 8 in reply to Salisbury's contained a sentence about
the colonial disputes—" Our colonial questions are to my
great satisfaction nearly regulated and their final settlement is close at hand "[2]—startlingly reminiscent of those
earlier final settlements, which had been the prelude to
fresh demands and quarrels.

Of greater importance were the developments in France,
where the impending elections (due in October) produced a
good deal of flamboyant nationalist propaganda. Freycinet
remained in office, but the strength of the anti-German
feeling had been shown, and by October it needed no great
prescience to expect the rise of the Boulangist movement,
which could hardly have been foreseen in May. In these
circumstances it was useless for Freycinet to argue that his
policy remained the same;[3] Bismarck recognised Freycinet's pacific intentions, but he had no longer the hope of
appeasing French public opinion.[4] But the decisive event

[1] Münster to the German Foreign Office, telegram, June 26, 1885.
G.P. vol. iv. No. 770, p. 131 ; Salisbury to Bismarck, private, July 2,
1885. G.P. vol. iv. No. 782, pp. 132-3.

[2] Bismarck to Salisbury, July 8, 1885. G.P. vol. iv. No. 783, pp.
133-4.

[3] In conversation with Hohenlohe. Freycinet to Courcel, very
confidential, Oct. 1, 1885. D.D.F. vol. vi. No. 79, pp. 95-8 ; and instructions to Courcel, Oct. 17, 1885. D.D.F. vol. vi. No. 96, pp. 115-17.

[4] Courcel to Ferry, confidential, Oct. 22, 1885. D.D.F. vol. vi. No.

was neither in France nor in England; it was in Philippo-
polis. On September 18, 1885, a rebellion broke out in
Eastern Roumelia ; and on September 20 Prince Alexander
of Bulgaria announced the union of Eastern Roumelia with
Bulgaria. The Eastern Question was reopened. For the sake
of Austria-Hungary, Bismarck could no longer afford to
estrange England, and as early as September 28 Bismarck
was belittling the colonial disputes as window-dressing to
attract the French.[1] The Franco-German *rapprochement*
had been an experiment, only made possible by the quies-
cence of the Near East ; that had now come to an end
and the danger of a Franco-Russian alliance had to be
averted, if that were possible, by other means than a
Franco-German alliance against England.

103, pp. 127-30. Cf. Bismarck to Hohenlohe, Sept. 21, 1885. G.P. vol.
iii. No. 707, p. 452.

[1] Currie, memorandum of conversation with Bismarck, Sept. 28,
1885. Cecil, *Salisbury*, vol. iii. p. 257.

EPILOGUE

THE only unsettled colonial question was East Africa, which provided an excuse for disputes between the two countries whenever the European situation called for them. The Salisbury ministry of 1885 was treated tolerantly by Bismarck, as he expected Salisbury to revive the policy of 1878 and co-operate with Austria-Hungary, and the question of Zanzibar was not mentioned. In the spring of 1886 there was a temporary lull in the Eastern Question and a new Gladstone ministry in England, which—despite having Rosebery at the Foreign Office—showed little inclination to support Austria-Hungary. For the last time there was a *rapprochement* between Germany and France, though Bismarck was a good deal more sceptical about it than in the previous year,[1] and the quarrels between the local agents in Zanzibar gave Bismarck an opening to threaten England with German hostility in Egypt and the Near East.[2] However, the approach to France was not very promising, and it was really useless to try to pick a colonial quarrel with the Gladstone government, which was completely absorbed in home affairs. The disputes in Zanzibar were therefore once more forgotten.

At the end of July 1886 Salisbury again assumed office and retained it until 1892, though he did not take over the Foreign Office until early in 1887. The French now made another attempt to settle the Egyptian question. They approached the English with the suggestion that

[1] Courcel to Freycinet, March 26, 1886. D.D.F. vol. vi. No. 217, pp. 224-9.

[2] Herbert Bismarck to Hatzfeldt, March 19, 1886. G.P. vol. iv. No. 790, p. 143; Bismarck to Hatzfeldt, April 21, 1886. G.P. vol. iv. No. 792, pp. 145-7.

England should withdraw from Egypt and that in return France would support England against Russia in Bulgaria ; [1] at the same time they approached Germany for support against England in the Egyptian question.[2] Bismarck had now, with the growth of the Boulangist movement, lost all faith in the possibility of a Franco-German entente; on the other hand, he was very anxious to see an agreement between France and England, which would leave England much freer to oppose Russia and so relieve the pressure on Austria.[3] The time was therefore opportune for a settlement of the Zanzibar question, which would show France she had nothing to hope for from Germany. The discussion was opened in the usual way with exaggerated German threats (September 29) ; [4] but Bismarck made it clear that he wanted to get the question out of the way and an agreement was reached on October 29. A dividing line was drawn between the German and British spheres of influence on the mainland, and an attempt was made to define the actual territory of the Sultan of Zanzibar. The agreement was not a final settlement, as the division of the hinterland was not complete, and subsequent dispute also arose over the status of the Sultan of Witu, whom the British regarded as subordinate to the Sultan of Zanzibar and the Germans as an independent prince.

However, for the moment all was perfect. The negotiations between England and France did not lead to any result, but England took up an increasingly resolute attitude in the Near East, which culminated in the exchange

[1] Waddington to Freycinet, Nov. 3, 1886. D.D.F. vol. vi. No. 342, p. 346 ; Nov. 23, 1886, No. 358, p. 372.

[2] Herbert Bismarck to William I., Sept. 28, 1886. G.P. vol. iv. No. 1227, pp. 137-8.

[3] Memorandum by Rantzau, Oct. 22, 1886. G.P. vol. iv. No. 803, p. 156 ; memorandum by Bismarck, Nov. 19, 1886. G.P. vol. iv. No. 806, p. 162.

[4] Memorandum by Rantzau, Sept. 29, 1886. G.P. vol. iv. No. 797, pp. 150-51.

of Notes between Italy and England on February 12, 1887, and the subsequent adhesion of Austria-Hungary on March 23, 1887. One part of Bismarck's problem, the strengthening of Austria-Hungary without German assistance, was thus solved; the other part, keeping Russia and France separated, remained. For a moment he seems to have thought once more of Franco-German co-operation, and on March 26 (three days after the exchange of letters between Austria-Hungary and England) threatened to support France in Egypt in revenge for the unfriendly attitude of British officials in Zanzibar.[1] But the time for such a policy had long since passed, and Bismarck cannot have taken the idea very seriously.

More promising was an agreement between Germany and Russia, by which Russia would be kept apart from France in return for German support in the Near East. The idea of a secret arrangement of this kind seems to have been first mooted by Giers, the Russian Foreign Minister, on April 13, 1887,[2] and it was an idea which was very welcome to Bismarck. Germany—this was a cardinal point in his policy—had no interests of her own in the Near East, and he had repeatedly told the Austrians that they must not count on German support for their Near Eastern plans. The only difficulty lay with England. Bismarck had certainly told the English that Germany would herself take no action in the Near East, but he had done his utmost to encourage the co-operation between England, Italy, and Austria-Hungary, and had undoubtedly given the English the impression that Germany approved of the objects of this Triple Entente. If Germany now began to support Russian claims concerning Bulgaria and the Straits—still worse, if Russia (as was quite conceivable) subsequently

---

[1] Herbert Bismarck to Hatzfeldt, March 26, 1887. G.P. vol. iv. Nos. 809 and 810, pp. 165-8; Herbette (ambassador at Berlin) to Freycinet, March 26, 1887. D.D.F. vol. vi. No. 483, p. 492.

[2] Bülow to Bismarck, April 14, 1887. G.P. vol. v. No. 1072, p. 222.

revealed the terms of the secret agreement to England—
would not the English feel that they had been deceived
and betrayed ? The Reinsurance Treaty (as the agreement
between Russia and Germany was later called) needed itself
to be insured against on the English side. There was an
obvious solution : to tell England, before the Reinsurance
Treaty was made, that English unfriendliness in Zanzibar
was driving Germany to be more friendly to Russia. This
simple precaution was taken by Bismarck at the end of
April 1887, a fortnight after the Russian approach ; the
complaints were of the most trivial kind and were at once
rectified by Salisbury, but the demonstration was now
safely recorded in case of subsequent difficulties.[1]

Colonial disputes between England and Germany were
now, for some time, at an end. England drew steadily closer
to Austria-Hungary and Italy, without complaining of the
German reserve ; Russian hostility to Germany was not
long appeased by the Reinsurance Treaty ; and French
hostility to Germany became ever more outspoken. By the
beginning of 1889 Bismarck was contemplating a new com-
bination—an Anglo-German alliance against France ; this
would strengthen England in Egypt and, by making France
an undesirable ally, bring Russia on to better terms with
Germany.[2] This idea had probably little attraction for
Salisbury: England, he believed, could settle with France
alone, nor did he desire a permanent estrangement between
the two countries ; it was against Russia that he needed
support and there Germany would not help him. When
Herbert Bismarck came over to England in March 1889,
Salisbury gave a negative, though friendly, answer, explain-

[1] Bismarck to Plessen [chargé d'affaires], telegram, April 27, 1887.
G.P. vol. iv. No. 812, pp. 169-70 ; Herbert Bismarck to Plessen, April
28, 1887. G.P. vol. iv. No. 813, pp. 170-71 ; Plessen to Foreign Office,
telegram, April 28, 1887. G.P. vol. iv. No. 814, p. 171 ; Bismarck to
Plessen, April 29, 1889. G.P. vol. iv. No. 815, p. 172.

[2] Bismarck to Hatzfeldt, Jan. 11, 1889. G.P. vol. iv. No. 943,
pp. 400-402.

ing that English public opinion was not ready for any continental alliance.[1] Herbert Bismarck also saw his friend Chamberlain, who, though not in office, was in a position of outstanding importance as the leading Liberal Unionist ; Chamberlain was very anxious for Anglo-German co-operation and seems to have suggested an exchange of German South-West Africa for Heligoland, as a demonstration of Anglo-German friendship.[2] Herbert welcomed the idea, but Salisbury apparently thought that he was being offered in South-West Africa a liability rather than an asset, and the suggestion was not pursued.[3] The young Emperor William II. was due to visit England in August 1889 and wished to celebrate his visit by some striking act ; in June he proposed to Bismarck that the Heligoland bargain should be revived,[4] but Bismarck did not wish to hurry matters, particularly as the Cape Colony was at this moment disliked in England and an arrangement which brought it more territory would have no good effect on English public opinion.[5] William II. was persuaded to leave the matter alone and to content himself with being made an English Admiral.

The suggestion of using Heligoland as a bargaining counter had not been lost on Salisbury, though he was uninterested in German South-West Africa; his attention was concentrated on the Nile valley, and he was anxious that German influence should not be added there to the rivalry of France, Belgium, Italy, and Abyssinia. In December

---

[1] Herbert Bismarck to Bismarck, March 22, 1889. G.P. vol. iv. No. 945, p. 405.

[2] Herbert Bismarck to Bismarck, March 27, 1889. G.P. vol. iv. No. 946, pp. 407-9.

[3] Hatzfeldt to Bismarck, April 13, 1880. G.P. vol. iv. No. 949, pp. 411-12.

[4] Berchem to Bismarck, June 21, 1889. G.P. vol. iv. No. 951, pp. 413-14.

[5] Herbert Bismarck to Berchem, June 21, 1889. G.P. vol. iv. No. 952, pp. 415-17 ; Bismarck to Foreign Office, June 23, 1889. G.P. vol. iv. No. 953, p. 417.

1889 he proposed that their East African disputes should be submitted to arbitration;[1] but nothing was done until after the fall of Bismarck, when the way of direct negotiation was chosen. On May 13, 1890, Salisbury put before Hatzfeldt proposals which became the basis for a complete settlement on June 14. The frontier of German East Africa was to be so drawn as to exclude the Germans from contact with the Nile valley; the Germans gave up their patronage of the Sultan of Witu, and England was to be allowed to assume the protectorate of Zanzibar; in return England would induce the Sultan of Zanzibar to renounce all authority over the German territory on the mainland, and would surrender Heligoland to Germany.[2] The German statesmen—Caprivi, the new Chancellor, and Marschall, the new Secretary—accepted these proposals with enthusiasm : they would receive additional territory in Africa and, much more important, they would receive Heligoland; this would make the agreement popular in Germany and would be very valuable for the future German fleet, of which William II. was already dreaming. It is true that they would give up something—a useful topic for disputes with England and, in the access to the Nile, a means of exercising pressure on England.

But the men of the " New Course " were not thinking of disputes with England. In their opinion Bismarck's policy, with its checks and balances, its insurances and reinsurances, had been far too complicated. Their views, in the early summer of 1890, were still very crude—Russia, they believed, was inevitably set on war, and no diplomatic manœuvre could stop her ; Germany must pledge herself unreservedly to Austria and must bring England into the Triple Alliance (that she had hitherto failed to do this was ascribed to the equivocal policy Bismarck had pursued

---

[1] Hatzfeldt to Bismarck, Dec. 22, 1889. G.P. vol. vi. No. 1674, pp. 6-8.

[2] Hatzfeldt to Marschall, May 14, 1890. G.P. vol. vi. No. 1676, pp. 11-14.

towards Russia and to his general incompetence); French hostility towards Germany would disappear with the fall of Bismarck, and in any case France would be so over-awed by the strength of the Triple Alliance and England combined that she would beg to be admitted. The Zanzibar-Heligoland treaty was the open demonstration that Germany had come out on the anti-Russian side, and was intended to be the prelude to the Quadruple Alliance of England, Germany, Italy, and Austria-Hungary.

With the passage of time the new German statesmen were to learn that their political calculations had been wrong, and their contempt for Bismarck and his apprehensions unjustified. England did not join the Triple Alliance; France was not appeased; and Russia, in her isolation, was driven into a co-operation with France which eventually produced the Franco-Russian alliance. The Germans were later to revise their plans; they were to approach Russia and even France once more, and to discover new disputes with England. Meanwhile, as the result of Bismarck's approach to France and quarrel with England, they were left with a number of expensive colonies and with one colony (the Cameroons) which was conceivably worth having; they were also left with the island of Heligoland, which was certainly worth having, but which Bismarck would probably have been able to obtain without having to pay the price of a Franco-Russian alliance. It is no discredit to Bismarck that in pursuit of his aims he used means that were as unscrupulous as they were elaborate. In Friedjung's words: *Sein Bild wird durch die geschichtliche Wahrheit keinen Abbruch erfahren* (Bismarck can stand the truth, warts and all). But he left an unfortunate example to his successors, who imitated his unscrupulousness without possessing his genius. Short of a run of Bismarcks, there is perhaps something to be said for government by gentlemen, even when they are such incompetent muddlers as Lord Granville and Lord Derby.

INDEX

Abyssinia, 9, 97

Afghanistan, 1, 81

Africa, 2, 32, 34; Berlin conference concerning, 47, 51, 72

Alexander II., 19

Algiers, 19

Alsace-Lorraine, 1, 11, 13, 31

Ampthill, Lord, 5, 22, 29, 40, 42, 46, 47, 67; death, 49 *n.*

Angra Pequena, German concession at, 23-4; British refusal to annex, 28; placed under German protection, 33; Anglo-German dispute over, 38-40; settlement of dispute, 41-2; dispute revived, 46. *See also* German South-West Africa

Annam, 1

Australia, 67

Austria-Hungary, 7, 9, 10, 13, 17, 18, 19, 52, 81, 92, 93, 95, 96

Barrère, Camille, 52

Bismarck, Count Herbert, unsatisfactory conduct of negotiations by, 22, 41, 42, 78; his opinion of German South-West Africa, 56; visit to England in June 1884, 41-2; in September 1884, 57; in March 1885, 78-9; in March 1889, 96-7; visit to France in October 1884, 58-9; letter to Granville, August 30, 1884, 51-2, 53, 56

Bismarck, Prince Otto, seeks reconciliation with France (December 1883), 20; prepares quarrel with England, 26; proposes Franco-German league against England (April 1884), 30-31; offers friendship of Germany to England (May 1884), 33-5; quarrels with England, 38-40; is reconciled to England, (June 1884), 42-4; proposes Franco-German entente against England

and revives Anglo-German dispute (August 1884), 46-9; advocates league against England (September 1884), 53-4; refuses to support France against England (November 1884), 61; makes new approach to France, 62-4; finds new ground for quarrel with England (December 1884), 69-75; is reconciled to England (March 1885), 77-9; approves of Russian plans in central Asia, 81; proposes continental league against England (May 1885), 83-4; abandons attempt at Franco-German entente, 87-90; his use of the Zanzibar question (1885–90), 92-6

attitude to colonies, 4-5, 23, 26

opinion of Gladstone, 19, 30, 59, 61, 62-3, 79

dispatch of May 5, 1884, 33-6

Bleichroeder, 29, 75

Boer republics, 1, 2, 3, 11

Bülow, 13

Cameroons, 3, 32, 66, 78, 99

Cape Colony, 2, 3, 23, 25, 28, 33, 38, 43, 97

Caprivi, 98

Chamberlain, Joseph, 14, 57, 58, 71, 73, 97

China, 1, 6, 12, 51, 62, 63, 82

Congo Free State, 2, 9, 13; Anglo-Congolese treaty, 7-8

Continental league against England, proposals for, in 1884–5, 30, 46-9, 53-4, 62-4, 83-4; in 1896, 9

Courcel, 20, 30-31, 35, 37-8, 47-8, 50, 51, 53-4, 60, 83, 87-8, 90; on German hostility to England, 54, 73, 80; on French attitude to Germany, 64-5, 90

Crowe, Sir Eyre, 19, 33 *n.*, 81

THE END